MENDED

BEVERLEY BOOTHE

Published by Freiling Agency, LLC.

P.O. Box 1264
Warrenton, VA 20188

www.FreilingAgency.com

PB ISBN: 979-8-9897784-4-7
eBook ISBN: 979-8-9897784-5-4

Printed in the United States of America

Table of Contents

Introduction

THIS BOOK IS for individuals who have experienced the loss of an intimate relationship due to a breakup. Losing someone you are emotionally connected to can feel as if you are losing part of yourself. When you have opened up your heart to give and receive love in a relationship, and it ends, the loss can be unbearable. This book will provide guidance in how to emotionally and spiritually heal so you can open up your heart to love again. The loss may be due to a divorce or the end of a committed relationship. It will help you explore why your relationship ended, understand the baggage that each person brings to a relationship from childhood, learn the importance of forgiveness to be free, and regain the strength to love and receive love from a purpose partner.

This book will highlight my journey of love and loss and the experiences of people I have counseled over the years. There will be a discussion about the stages of grief and how to go through them to get to the place of acceptance of a breakup. Understanding each person's contribution to the ending of the relationship will help in the healing process. Being honest with where you are in the healing journey will help you explore your feelings and know that you have the ability to get through every obstacle and trial. You need to know that you are not alone and have the strength to overcome every challenge life throws at you, even when your relationship falls apart. We all go through situations in life that are difficult and painful, but with perseverance and courage, the obstacles can be overcome.

This book is for you if you are ready to move past your hurt and pain and to reclaim your dreams of having a healthy relationship. If you are willing to identify the areas of your life in which you keep getting stuck so you can break free, then this book is also for you. It takes courage to trust again and be vulnerable, but with hope and faith, you can get through the healing process to experience the love you deserve. This book will also help you learn the steps to heal from heartbreak successfully. Relying on a Source outside yourself will enable you to step into the unknown until you get to the other side of the healing process.

This book is about faith, perseverance, forgiveness, love, intentionality, and resilience. It's about looking at your life in a new way with renewed hope, despite your

SAHHHHH

77777

circumstances. Let's begin the journey together if you are ready to heal, live whole, and love again.

.

Part I

The Desire of Connection

The Dream of a Partner

WE ARE RELATIONAL beings. In other words, human beings have an innate desire to be in relationships with others. Although 85 percent of people will marry within their lifetimes, approximately 50 percent of these marriages will end in divorce. Despite these statistics, most people continue to hope that they will find compatible partners. Numerous relationship books are available, yet romantic relationships continue to fail. It has always made me curious why people struggle to have long-lasting relationships even with a plethora of information about how to make a marriage or committed relationship work. Here are some questions to be considered:

- What makes some marriages or committed partnerships last and others fail?
- Why do some people hold on to relationships even though they see red flags?

- Why don't we take the time to heal our baggage before we enter into romantic relationships?
- Why is it difficult for some people to leave toxic relationships?
- Why are the infidelity rates so high?
- Why do people continue to dream of finding new relationships, even after toxic breakups?

My work as a licensed psychotherapist has made me ponder these questions. I have seen couples who are successful in saving their relationships and couples who choose to walk away after therapy. It's essential to understand how our thoughts, feelings, and behaviors impact how we relate to others and the outcome we often receive. Whatever the experience, almost everyone continues to dream of finding a partner who will provide a sense of connection, safety, and oneness.

Childhood Wounds

As a little girl, I imagined finding the perfect man I would eventually marry. I believed it would happen someday as long as I stayed in God's will. Even though I wanted to get married, I also feared it. My only example of marriage was my parents. Growing up, I saw them struggle in their relationship, and I did not want a marriage like theirs.

My parents were married for over fifty years, but their relationship was difficult. I remember hearing them argue regularly. My dad had indiscretions, which devastated my mother. It deeply hurt her, but she stayed in the marriage because she felt she could not leave with four children. My mother was very proud and private. She did not want people to know that my dad had multiple affairs. He also had a child outside of marriage, which emotionally crushed my mother. Although my siblings and I became aware of the affairs, we did not discuss the subject because it was taboo in our home. I found out about the affairs because I heard my parents arguing about them.

I remember seeing a picture of a little girl on the fireplace mantel, and I assumed from overhearing conversations that she was my half sister. When I was about ten years old, I asked my mother, "Who is the girl in the picture?"

Her response was, "Go ask your dad."

I asked my dad the same question. He responded, "When you get older, I will let you know."

Even though I knew the answer to the question since I had already figured it out, I just wanted them to talk about it.

My parents' marital struggles impacted the entire family. I eventually realized that my father had unresolved childhood wounds that needed to be healed. My mother also had a difficult childhood from being raised in a home where there was infidelity. I greatly admire my mother's strength to remain in a marriage where she was unfulfilled because of her love for her children.

Unfortunately, many couples' marriages end in divorce due to a partner being unfaithful. Infidelity occurs at an alarming rate in relationships, and it is one of the leading causes of divorce. Unfortunately, 40 to 50 percent of all couples will experience infidelity in their relationships. When infidelity is experienced, the relationship deteriorates due to broken trust and feelings of shame, anger, despair, or betrayal in the betrayed partner and sometimes feelings of guilt in the betrayer. Navigating through the grief of infidelity is a complicated process. When a couple decides to remain in the marriage despite the infidelity, the work to repair the relationship and rebuild trust is complex.

When my parents argued, they stopped speaking with each other for days or weeks at a time. I often found myself trying to support both of them. I did not want to see the hurt in my mother's eyes or experience the continual tension in the household. I often felt that it was best if my parents did not stay together.

I remember my mother telling me, "I think I'm going to leave your father." I knew I would choose to stay with her if she left him. I understood her decision because they were so unhappy in their relationship. However, my mother chose to stay. Since they had a difficult time emotionally connecting with each other and their marriage was so strained, I vowed to find a partner with whom I could have a different experience.

My dad was a provider. He worked hard as a general contractor. I knew he loved his family but had difficulty communicating his feelings. He was kind but did not know how to express his love verbally. I remember, at age thirteen, making a decision to understand my dad better. I decided I had to learn to communicate with him since he did not know how to express himself to us. This decision helped me to feel more connected to my dad. I finally heard the words "I love you" as an adult while leaving home for college. Therefore, I spent several years praying that I would marry a man that would be a good communicator. I found myself having difficulty being vulnerable in relationships because I was afraid to marry a man who would not remain faithful or did not know how to express his feelings.

I have come to understand how important it is to understand our childhood stories and their impact on our romantic relationships. We cannot divorce ourselves from our childhood experiences. Psychiatrist John Bowlby expressed that we experience four attachment styles as children. They are anxious, avoidant, disorganized, and secure styles. These attachment styles will influence how we relate to our partners. Children with anxious, avoidant, or disorganized attachment styles often have difficulties with healthy attachments in their romantic relationships. The hope is to have a secure style as a child to attach to an intimate partner successfully. I had a mother who created emotional security in my life and a father who struggled with emotional connection. I had to understand my parents' roles in my life to work on my emotional healing journey.

Waiting for the Vision to Manifest

I envisioned a marriage that would last forever. Since I was goal-oriented, I wrote down all the qualities I wanted in a relationship. As a Christian, I held onto the scripture that states, "Write the vision, and make it plain" (Habakkuk 2:2).

My pastor at the time encouraged me to write down the vision and goals I wanted in marriage. I kept this list as my guide to meeting the man I felt would be my forever husband. When most of my friends married in their twenties and it wasn't happening for me, I continued to hope and dream that my soulmate would show up. I dated a few men, but they were not right for me because each relationship fell apart due to incompatibility. I just continued to dream and held on to my relationship list.

I remember meeting Darryl at church. He appeared to be the perfect guy for me. He was a talented musician and a dynamic individual. I thought I loved him, but he did not love me in return. He did not commit to a relationship; however, I kept hoping he would miraculously fall in love with me. He was not there for me when I needed him to remember my birthday or when I wanted him to attend my graduation. I kept forgiving him and waiting for him to realize that I was the "best" woman for him. I did not know that he was spending time with another young woman in our church who also had strong feelings for him. When I finally found out, that still was not enough for me to end our involvement. I kept hoping and dreaming that he would see my value. I finally woke up when I went to his apartment unannounced to find another young woman from our church there. I was devastated. It finally woke me up. I realized that I was not valuing myself. Even though I eventually moved on, I had to grieve the loss. It took me a couple of years of regularly reminding myself that I should not settle for less than I deserve.

I moved away from the area and threw myself into studying to occupy my mind versus addressing my emotions. The only way I knew how to heal back then was to keep busy.

Faith Jenkins' book, *Sis, Don't Settle*, reminds us that women should know their worth and not settle for relationships out of desperation.

How many people see red flags, ignore them, and continue full speed ahead? My female clients would tell me that they have had boyfriends and husbands who continually cheated on them, physically and verbally abused them, did not show up when they were sick, and showed complete disrespect for them, but they continued to hope that they would change. Some people have learned that having a "partner" is better than remaining single. Oftentimes when you open your heart, it is difficult to walk away even when logic tells you that this is not the right partner for you. We also have seen our family members and friends model that it's okay to hold on to a relationship when it's unhealthy. We must remember to break these unhealthy patterns that keep us stuck. It's time that as individuals we understand our worth.

I teach my clients the importance of having a vision of what they want in their lives. I tell them to envision their goals being manifested. I ask them to develop a vision board and to be specific in outlining how their goals will happen. I also encourage them to draw multiple circles and write down the specific qualities they want in a relationship. I believe in the importance of speaking into existence the desires of your heart. Scripture says, "You have not because you ask not" (James 4:2). When we write down the desires of our hearts and pray for what we want, we will see it manifested if it is aligned with God's purpose for our lives. We often do not know what we desire because we are afraid to hope and walk in faith to receive it.

I also tell my clients that to manifest the relationships of their dreams; they must first know themselves. It's impossible to dream about who is best for you if you don't know who you are. Looking back, I didn't really know who I was in my twenties. I knew I wanted to meet someone honest and faithful, but I did not understand the effort needed to have a thriving and resilient relationship. We need a level of maturity to understand who is best for us. Even more important is knowing who God has for us. I desired to have a relationship with a man with whom I would have a physical, emotional, and spiritual connection. I also wanted a relationship with a man who was a good communicator and who was living with integrity and a strong Christian faith. I learned that manifesting a partner who was right for me meant that I had to listen to the small voice inside that would tell me that he was the one.

Writing down your desires and praying for each of these qualities will help to manifest them. Secondly, you should write down the specifics of what you want in a relationship. Be clear about the characteristics you desire in your partner. Think about what you desire in the short term and the future. Remember, you must know who you are to identify the qualities you want in a partner. Keep in mind that even though you may be able to identify a vision for your relationship, God may have a different plan for you if your vision for a partner does not align with His will.

Thirdly, if you want to manifest the relationship of your dreams, you and your partner must do internal work to heal wounds from childhood and past relationships. This is such a critical process for your relationship to thrive. Many people think the romantic love and passionate feelings they are experiencing will last forever. However, the newness will soon fade. You will soon discover that the partner who you have fallen in love with also comes with a set of experiences that will show up in the romantic relationship. When you take the time to understand your story and how it has impacted your view of yourself and the world, you will be more prepared to make your relationship work. This awareness allows you to show up whole rather than look for someone else to complete you.

Overlooking the Red Flags

When you meet the person you feel that God has brought into your life, a decision needs to be made about how to date or court each other with the intention of making the relationship permanent. The courtship phase can be special because both parties are intentional in showing the best of themselves. It is even more special when you have waited and prayed for a spouse or partner and see that person manifest.

I met my husband in my mid-thirties and we married three years later. I wanted to find the man that God had for me; however, it was taking longer than I thought it should. I kept waiting and praying for God to send the right person. I wanted to have a marriage that was glorifying to God and to be an example to other couples. Although I had hoped to get married in my twenties, I was also afraid to marry someone God did not have for me since I did not have good relationship models growing up.

I was drawn to my husband because I thought he was the male version of my personality. We appeared to have so much in common. He was extremely kind and affectionate. I felt that I was a priority in his life. He thought about my needs and did thoughtful acts without me asking. Since church and my faith were important to me, he attended church regularly with me. We traveled together. Everything felt like a fairy tale.

Despite our connection, I was still afraid to be vulnerable during the initial courtship phase of our relationship. Since I waited so long to commit to someone fully, I was hoping this was the person God had for me. Our relationship initially had a few ups and downs, but we appeared to connect well. I was concerned because he was married previously, and the relationship with his ex-wife ended due to infidelity. He assured me that he had changed, and that was out of character for him. I was able to let go of my fears and open up my heart to him due to our level of connection as friends and romantic partners. I learned to trust and be vulnerable with him and decided that I was ready to marry him.

Right before we got married, I discovered that he was not completely honest about essential details of his previous marriage. Although I felt betrayed by him and realized that his omission of information was a red flag, I felt that I had invested three years of my life that I didn't want to lose. We got through the process by attending one couple's counseling session, which was insufficient. Even though I was hurt, I decided to move forward in our relationship because I thought the pain of letting him go would be worse.

When I committed to marrying him, I stopped doubting the relationship. I convinced myself that this was the man that God chose for me. I felt very ready to say yes and commit my life to him. I felt completely in love and grateful for being able to start this phase of my life. We attended premarital counseling through my church; however, I realized we rushed the six-month process because we felt we were mature and understood marriage and commitment. Although I had lingering concerns about the omission of information discovered about his previous relationship, I decided to move forward in preparing for our marriage.

Real Love or Fairy-Tale Relationship

Nearly every girl dreams of finding a soulmate and wearing the perfect wedding dress for walking down the aisle to say, "I do." She hopes for a man who has the ability to "sweep her off her feet" and have a happily-ever-after fairy-tale ending. When I finally married, I felt our love would never fail. We became an example for other couples in our church and became the couples' ministry leaders. We were also the couple that our family members looked up to, and many people desired a marriage like ours. We worked on establishing goals for our marriage, reviewed them periodically, and established new ones when we accomplished those we developed together. We also traveled to various places on our anniversaries to experience new adventures together. I thought my life was perfect. However, I soon learned that the wedding day can be a fairy tale, but marriage has numerous ups and downs. Marriage will survive only when both individuals understand the gravity of the work to make the marriage thrive.

My marriage seemed extremely easy and fun. We had minimal conflict and saw eye to eye on most issues. I felt secure in the relationship and trusted my husband fully. I completely let my guard down and loved him with all my heart. I thought, "Nothing can come between us." He thanked me for trusting him and believing in him to take care of our marriage as a protector. I thought the work we put in to make our marriage thrive would end in "until death does us part." But, unfortunately, this wasn't our story.

I went through a period of darkness when my fairy-tale marriage came crashing down. After ten years of marriage and over three years of dating, I discovered that my spouse was not living authentically and was unfaithful in the marriage. The red flags I saw before we got married became my reality. The lies that were discovered left me broken and afraid. I didn't know how I would recover from this level of pain.

I was in a dark place and felt very alone. My best friend and partner had betrayed me. I not only lost my husband and friend, but I also lost my direction and joy. It propelled me into a life of prayer and faith. I had to depend on God because my life depended on it.

I didn't know how to survive financially, but I knew that God's Word said, "Be anxious for nothing, but give thanks in everything" (Philippians 4:6). My marriage became strained because the trust I had in my spouse was broken. I tried to make sense of what went wrong. I could not reconcile the betrayal, so we grew distant, and our marriage eventually fell apart.

I struggled with the shame of seeking a divorce because I feared what people would say or think, especially since I was a marriage therapist. I didn't want anyone to know that my marriage was falling apart; however, I knew it was time to walk away from it. Despite my pain, I had to keep moving forward to care for myself and our child, who was a toddler at the time. I stayed in the marriage for two more years after it shattered to grieve the loss and to rebuild myself financially. I had to learn how to appreciate the bad experiences and cherish the good ones to rise above the obstacles I was experiencing.

If you live long enough, you will experience at least one emotional breakup. Since you were born to be connected to others, you will learn that you can feel lonely, isolated, and lost without connections. Therefore, you may seek relationships with people you can relate to and feel safe with. You desire for them to love you and for you to give your love in return.

There is a sense of vulnerability when you open your heart so that you can be known. Having this sense of connection can be rich and rewarding. It helps you to grow emotionally and spiritually because you learn about yourself as you get to know your partner. However, what happens when this type of relationship ends? Not every relationship will last a lifetime. Some relationships are seasonal and will therefore eventually come to an end. Sometimes a broken relationship feels like a piece of your heart has been ripped away.

I discovered that I had to learn the importance of letting go of shame because I was trying very hard to have a marriage that was an example to others. Since shame weighed me down, it created depression and loneliness in my life. I was too ashamed to tell others outside my family what I was experiencing. I told one person at my church but did not receive the support I needed.

You cannot triumph through adversity until you release the shame and guilt that hold you back. The fear of being judged can keep you stuck and alone. Some people may judge you, but if they do, it's time to release them from your life. You have to surround yourself with people who will show you unconditional love and support.

When I finally opened up to a few people, I discovered their incredible friendship. I learned the importance of not judging others since we do not like being judged. It's easy to condemn others without having the whole story, or sometimes we make up our own stories about their misfortunes. We fail to look at our dysfunction or to understand someone else's pain because we see things from our own perspective. There is always a lesson to be learned from your struggles and failures. Letting go of your shame enables you to use your experiences to help others experiencing similar pain.

After two years of living in pain and holding on to shame after finding out the truth about the man I married, I finally decided to move beyond my circumstances and walk away from the marriage. I had to return to the life God called me to live. I remember praying twenty years before for God to use me. I asked Him to help me live a life of surrender to Him. I realized that whatever circumstances occurred in my life, I had to trust God that if He allowed me to experience it, He would bring me through it. I also realized that in His infinite wisdom, everything was orchestrated to allow me to fully rely on Him emotionally, financially, physically, and spiritually. He gave me a new purpose and fight. I had to rely on God to help me in my healing journey.

Part II

The Journey of Discovery

The Pain of a Broken Relationship

LIKE SO MANY people, when you walk down the aisle to exchange marriage vows, you probably imagine it will last the rest of your life. Hardly anyone would enter a marriage thinking it will be seasonal. I thought the relationship I had was going to be a lifetime. When the marriage fell apart, my heart broke. I didn't know how I would make it through the dark period. I couldn't see the light amid my darkness. I went through a period of grief before moving to a place of acceptance.

I spent several years trying to determine what went wrong in my relationship. I was doing everything correctly. We established goals, communicated daily, attended church together, had date nights, and vacationed together. We weren't supposed to end. I found myself questioning everything I believed in.

I wanted to stop counseling couples since my marriage did not work. However, couples kept calling me for services. I ran into a client who said, "Thank you for saving my marriage." I was so happy for him, but I struggled with my loss. I remembered that I chose to say, "I do," despite the red flags I saw before I married. I chose not to walk away when I saw them because I feared not finding someone else who might be better. My journey of discovery led me back to school to specialize in marriage therapy to understand better what makes couples resilient. My research emphasized the importance of effective communication, having a shared belief system, healing past and current hurts, and making a commitment to rise above difficulties together.

I took the time to understand attachment theory to see how our childhood stories impact our current relationships. Since I was the responsible child growing up, and I attended to my parents during their struggles, I needed to understand how my childhood experiences impacted me. I realized that I wanted to shield my mother from her pain and support my father with his disconnection; however, I did not understand as a child that this was not my role but my parents' role to fix their marriage.

I married a man who lost his mother at the age of ten and was raised by a father who struggled to express his feelings. My ex-husband became the person that all his family members looked up to. He appeared strong and I did not see his insecurities. I finally felt that I could rely on an emotionally strong man so that I could let go of the heaviness of being strong for others. I did not see his insecurities and trusted him blindly. I quickly gave away the responsibilities I should have claimed, even when he said he wanted to take care of them. I allowed myself to let him lead with the assurance that he would never let me down. I looked to him for security rather than relying on my Creator. I had to get back to shifting my priorities to heal.

Emotional healing involves taking responsibility for your emotions and actively working to understand and resolve underlying issues. It's not just about feeling better; it's also about gaining the tools and skills to cope with life's challenges and developing a deeper under-standing of yourself. You must take the time to work on being emotionally healthy to be whole again after a breakup.

Fifteen Red Flags in Relationships

I mentioned earlier that I saw red flags in my rela-tionship, but I chose to get married anyway. Like me, many people have expressed that they saw red flags in their dating relationships, but they committed to moving forward in spite of them. A red flag is a warning sign that you are experiencing in the relationship, indicating a problem that may continue in the future. I have listed fifteen red flags that you need to consider before your relationship progresses and before you find it difficult to walk away. I saw some of these and chose to disregard them, and they eventually became more evident once I was married. This list is not exhaustive; however, the ones listed are important to consider before you say, "I do." Let's explore them.

1. *Dishonesty in the Relationship*

When you are in a dating relationship, and you realize that your partner is constantly telling you little lies or even big ones, it is a huge red flag. Honesty in a relationship is paramount to building trust. When trust has been damaged, it isn't easy to get it back. Dishonesty is not only about telling lies but also about the omission of pertinent information that might affect you. My ex-husband withheld information about his past when we were dating, which impacted me. This was a big red flag that I chose to overlook because we were already three years into the relationship. The news devastated me because it caused the beginning of distrust.

When your partner lies, you have to examine the underlying issues contributing to this. You have to determine if it is caused by a habit. Is it from a fear of hurting you or of making you angry by telling you the truth? Is your partner ashamed of a past decision and is now omitting the information? Your partner may condone the behavior and downplay the significance of telling you. Sometimes, your partner may be afraid of conflict and thinks it's better if you don't know the truth. Another reason may be the fear that you will withhold affection with this knowledge. Even still, your partner may feel a level of protection if you don't know the truth. Whatever the reasons, these examples are lies and dishonesty that will erode the relationship. Deception can prove detrimental to having a solid foundation unless it is addressed. If this is an issue in your relationship, please manage it before you move forward.

2. *Unresolved Past Baggage*

Let's face it: like anyone else, you have some level of trauma from childhood or from difficulties in romantic relationships. The question that you need to consider is whether or not the healing has been done. If you have committed to healing your past trauma and your partner has not, you will notice that your time and energy will be devoted to helping your partner heal. It's impossible to have a healthy relationship if you are functioning as your partner's therapist. This may create a codependency because the relationship is imbalanced, and boundaries become challenging to maintain. Codependency means that one person suppresses his or her own needs and emotions to focus on the partner's needs.

I worked with a couple who struggled in their marriage because the husband did not heal from his past relationship with his father, who had abandoned the family. He had difficulty committing emotionally to his wife, even though she tried to support him and to be patient as he tried to heal. She began to experience anxiety and depression in her quest to help him in his healing journey. She acknowledged that she saw her husband's struggles before they were married, but she committed herself to him despite the red flags. She thought that she could support him through his healing journey. She later decided to separate because she began to lose herself in trying to save him.

3. *Different Value Systems*

Research shows that couples can work through conflict more effectively if they have similar value systems. This does not necessarily mean that you have to belong to the same religion or have the same upbringing. A value system means you have specific goals, norms, or established values that you choose to live by. These values are essential to you, and you can't live authentically without them. If your partner does not agree with or value them, it will weaken your relationship.

I had a client who believed in being independent and wanted to work after her pregnancy. She married a man who was more traditional as the sole provider and wanted his wife to remain at home with the children. This posed a problem in their marriage, and they had difficulty navigating it.

It's important to know what both you and your partner value while dating. This will help you to be well-informed about whether or not there is compatibility in the relationship.

4. *Not Spiritually Aligned*

Similar to having different values, not being spiritually aligned can be a problem in a relationship. You are not spiritually aligned with your partner when he or she is critical of your beliefs, is uninterested in supporting your spiritual practice, or judges you when you engage in it. Sometimes you and your partner have similar religious core values and both believe in God; however, you may desire to attend church each Sunday, but your partner is not interested in being a part of an organized religion and won't participate with you. These behaviors will cause feelings of hurt and disconnection, contributing to red flags in the relationship.

Jackie and Jeremy met each other through mutual friends. Jackie was raised a Christian, and Jeremy was raised a Muslim. They fell in love and soon married. Jackie was concerned that Jeremy had a different religion and hoped it would not affect their relationship. When they had their first child, Jeremy wanted their son to be indoctrinated in the Muslim faith, and Jackie disagreed and wanted him to attend church. Since this became a constant disagreement in their home, Jackie conceded and stopped attending church altogether. The couple did not address the red flags before their wedding, which contributed to conflict after they were married.

5. *Emotional, Verbal, or Physical Abuse*

Abuse in a relationship is a huge red flag, and when this rears its ugly head, you should run away quickly. This varies from emotional abuse to a partner who controls, intimidates, manipulates, threatens, and demeans. You feel afraid when you are with your partner and not emotionally safe. Verbal abuse is when one partner uses words to intimidate, scare, insult, and control the other. This behavior may include excessive yelling or name-calling.

I worked with a young woman who was able to break free from an abusive relationship with her child's father. He was often controlling and jealous, which were big red flags for her. She stated that it quickly moved into verbal and physical abuse, and at times, she did not know if she would survive. She eventually found the strength to leave the relationship and to work through her healing process.

According to the Center for Disease Control and Prevention (CDC), approximately one in four women and one in seven men will experience physical violence at some point by an intimate partner. These are alarming numbers and can be reduced if more awareness is brought to this issue and individuals can walk away from partners who exhibit signs of abuse.

6. *Lack of Goals for Self*

When you are in a relationship, it's essential that your partner is clear about what he or she wants out of life and has direction and goals. If your partner feels lost, building a healthy relationship is difficult. Both of you should understand the direction you want to take in your lives and have a plan to accomplish it. If your partner doesn't, this can be a red flag, because his or her lack of direction can contribute to insecurities. Insecurities in an individual will contribute to insecurities in the relationship.

I met many individuals who feel stuck in their jobs but are afraid to try something new for various reasons. Feeling stuck can create undue stress in the individual and the relationship. Even though most people eventually figure out plans for their lives, waiting for a partner to have clarity can be very challenging, especially if the other partner has clarity.

7. *Substance Abuse Concerns*

Substance abuse is a mental health condition caused by excessive psychoactive drug use such as alcohol, illegal drugs, or pain medications that cause dependency. When one is dependent on these substances, it leads to issues in the relationship and is a huge red flag. When your partner has an addiction, building a healthy relationship is impossible. It's easy to develop a codependent relationship because you are trying to help your partner heal. Your partner must be the one who recognizes the need for help and seek professional support to break the addiction.

Gloria was married to Luke for twenty-five years, and there was a conflict in the marriage due to his addiction to cocaine. She tried to encourage him to go for help, but Luke was not ready. After attending a support group for family members of addicted partners, Gloria was able to find the strength to leave him. She realized that her marriage could not be saved without Luke seeking help for his disease. It's a tough decision to walk away from a loved one when he or she is in crisis, but it takes courage to walk away from emotional pain when you are in an unhealthy relationship.

8. *Keep Secrets*

It is a concern if your partner is afraid to talk about experiences that have occurred in the past and keeps secrets from you. Also, if he or she keeps you a secret after an extended period of dating, this is another red flag. Your partner may keep secrets out of fear that you will be upset if the truth were known. It is similar to the red flag that was previously discussed about dishonesty. Usually, the main reason for secrets is the fear of being judged. If your partner keeps you a secret, there may be a lack of commitment in the relationship. It's important to discuss why your partner is not opening up about significant issues or why he or she is keeping you a secret from others. If your partner cannot acknowledge the behavior, moving forward with the relationship can prove detrimental.

I met a young man who dated a girl for about three years. They eventually broke up because he was not ready to commit to marriage, and she was ready. He met someone else about six months later, but he did not introduce her to his family. He eventually broke up with her and reconciled with his first love. He said he did not introduce the second girl because he felt that she would not fit in with his family as his first girlfriend did. The second girlfriend was kept a secret. Understanding your partner's mindset is critical to knowing whether or not you should stay in a relationship.

9. *Constant Arguments*

Conflict is inevitable in a relationship and it enables a couple to grow. When two individuals come together with different life experiences, conflict will occur. Conflicts arise when needs or wishes are not aligned, and one or both individuals disagree. It is an opportunity to grow because both individuals must work on resolving the disagreement to maintain the relationship. However, conflicts will manifest in anger if a couple struggles to communicate needs in a healthy way. If a couple constantly argues and uses what researchers, Drs. John and Julie Gottman refer to as blame, sarcasm, stonewalling, or criticism rather than talking through the conflict, then this is a red flag in the relationship. Learning to communicate effectively through active listening and creating a safe space to share feelings are critical for an emotionally connected relationship.

I met a couple who had been dating for about six months. They often argued by yelling and blaming each other for their conflicts. They decided to get married after almost two years of dating but called it quits five years later due to poor communication. Communication issues should be dealt with early to help a couple work through conflict and grow in the relationship.

10. *Infidelity in the Relationship*

I mentioned earlier that many marriages end in divorce due to infidelity. This is when an individual in a committed relationship has an emotional or sexual relationship with another person who is not his or her partner. The impact of cheating in a relationship can be life-altering. It often creates feelings of anxiety, depression, and extreme stress for the betrayed partner. It breaks trust in the relationship, which can also lead to the breakdown of the family. Some couples can heal from it and move on with counseling. However, this is not an easy process to go through.

I met a couple whose marriage was struggling due to multiple affairs by the husband and later by the wife due to retaliation. The couple had trust issues with each other, which led to a lack of emotional intimacy. Infidelity is another big red flag, and you should consider the ramifications of continuing a relationship if it occurred with someone you just recently met. I have seen several women who knew that their partners cheated repeatedly during the dating phase but chose to marry anyway, hoping the behavior would change with a commitment. Remember that if a behavior happens before you get married, there is a high probability of it occurring afterwards. Underlying reasons must be addressed with a partner who cheats before you say, "I do!"

11. *Not a Priority in the Relationship*

When you are in a relationship and your partner is not interested in attending events that are important to you or focuses on meeting his or her own needs at the expense of yours, it is a red flag. Although it is essential to prioritize your need for self-care so that you can be emotionally available to others, if no time is devoted to the relationship, it will not grow.

I told you about my relationship with Darryl, who missed my birthday and graduation. He did not prioritize these events despite their significance in my life. It became clear that I was not a priority to him.

When you are a priority in the relationship, your partner will show up for you. He or she will create time and space to let you know your significance in the relationship. You don't have to demand to be a priority with a partner who understands your worth.

12. *Jealousy in the Relationship*

If your partner constantly expresses jealousy and tries to control who you spend time with or communicate with, this is a red flag. When your partner is jealous, this is a sign of insecurity, which means he or she is trying to control you in the relationship. When love resides, jealousy is not part of it. Feelings of jealousy are natural, but if your partner begins to control you because of them, it is unhealthy and a red flag.

I once worked with clients who were both previously married and met each other through an online dating app. They got along well and wanted to pursue a deeper relationship. Unfortunately, the man became jealous when the woman communicated with her ex-husband. Even though she explained that they were friends and both had moved on, he felt that she should have no contact with her ex-husband. He had no contact with his ex-spouse and had lingering anger toward her. He realized through counseling that he had to forgive his ex-wife and let go of controlling how his new girlfriend connected with her ex-husband.

13. *Unmanaged Mental Health Concerns*

Like the substance abuse red flag, an unmanaged mental health disorder can be problematic in building a healthy relationship. Examples of these issues are depression, severe anxiety, bipolar disorder, and others. When a disorder goes untreated, it's challenging to grow emotionally as a couple unless the affected partner seeks professional help.

When you are in a relationship, it's important to encourage your partner to get help if he or she is struggling with mental health concerns. If your partner refuses to get help, this red flag will prevent the relationship from thriving. Mental health disorders should be treated only by trained professionals. One partner in a relationship is not responsible for managing the other partner's mental health.

I worked with a client who married a man diagnosed with bipolar disorder. Although he sought treatment, which stabilized him, he later decided not to continue his medication. His wife was constantly anxious about changes in his mood and worried about when he would have an episode. She remained anxious due to living in a constant state of the unknown.

Understanding your partner's mental health history early in a new relationship is vital to determine if you want to continue growing in it.

14. *Lack of Sexual Chemistry*

When you meet a romantic partner and have a lack of sexual chemistry, this may pose an issue in the future. Sexual chemistry is having a physical attraction to your partner. Although having chemistry is essential, you can still fall in love with your partner without feeling physically attracted. Chemistry does not guarantee that you will fall in love with the other person; however, when you have, it will help in having a fulfilling relationship. When it exists at the beginning of your relationship, dopamine and other chemicals will cause you to connect with your partner. Often, if a couple doesn't have chemistry, the initial feeling of infatuation may not be present, which makes commitment more challenging. Although feelings of passion will fade over time, when chemistry was present initially, the couple will have the ability to work on it again. Sometimes, a couple may not have sexual chemistry, but the partners may experience feelings of emotional warmth and comfort that can contribute to good chemistry.

I have gone on dates with individuals with whom I have not experienced chemistry. I have learned not to pursue a relationship when the chemistry is not present to avoid issues in the future. If you do not experience a level of excitement and comfort with a partner when you initially meet, this is a big red flag, and more than likely, this is not the person you need to be with.

15. *Non-Commitment in the Relationship*

When a couple is committed to a relationship, the partners are dedicated to support each other now and in the future. Both partners desire to devote themselves to each other as a couple. You know your partner is committed when you discuss hopes and expectations for the future. You both make plans for strengthening the relationship and discuss goals for the future. If only one person is interested in this type of commitment, this is a red flag. Although this type of commitment would not be expected early in your relationship, it is expected when you are in a partnership for a significant time. Commitment involves two people who desire the same thing.

I worked with a couple who dated for a number of years and got along well as friends. The woman wanted to get married after ten years of dating, and they had two children together. He did not want to be married but wanted the relationship to continue because he did not want to be a part-time caretaker for their children. He expressed to her that he was not ready to propose and was unsure when he would be. The woman was left to decide whether to wait a few more years or to walk away. She saw the red flags early in the relationship when he did not propose, but she chose to live with him in the hope that it would lead to marriage. She was devastated when the marriage did not happen after ten years of being together. She realized that she should not have ignored the red flags.

The Grieving Process

Psychiatrist Elisabeth Kübler-Ross wrote about the five stages of grief that are typically experienced after the death of a loved one, which can provide insight into the complex emotions often endured at the end of a relationship. In addition, understanding the grieving stages provides a roadmap for checking in with your emotions and knowing how you're progressing toward recovery. These stages are denial, anger, bargaining, depression, and acceptance. While not everyone experiences these stages in the same order or with the same intensity, understanding these stages can help you recognize and cope with your emotions.

Stage 1: Denial

Denial is a defense mechanism in this early stage of grief, when you are in disbelief in your situation. You may struggle to accept that your relationship has died during this stage. This part of grieving is particularly hard and painful if you didn't see the breakup coming. When you've been completely blindsided, you'll assume that your partner will return or that the breakup is just a temporary setback. Also, when you're in this stage, you may ignore all the obvious signs that the relationship is over and may hold the hope that your relationship can thrive with a few changes. This can happen even when the relationship is unhealthy and toxic. It's important to understand that denial is a natural response to a breakup, and it is how your brain tries to protect itself from the pain of the loss. To move forward with your healing process, you'll eventually need to work through this stage by accepting the reality of the breakup.

Stage 2: Anger

Anger is the second stage, where you will look for a source to blame. This is often characterized by intense frustration, resentment, and even rage toward your ex-partner.

After a breakup or divorce, anger can manifest in many different ways. Some people become outwardly aggressive and lash out at their ex-partners or those around them. Others may become withdrawn and keep their emotions inside themselves. When you're going through this stage, you may feel as though you've been wronged, and you may struggle with feelings of betrayal or abandonment.

I dealt with my anger by keeping my feelings inside. Initially, I did not want to ever speak to my ex-husband again. I felt hurt, pain, and emotionally abandoned by him. I soon realized that I was not angry only with him but also with myself for my lack of awareness of the problems brewing in my marriage.

You may also get mad at yourself for not seeing the warning signs earlier, for not being strong enough to keep the relationship going, or for not ending the relationship sooner. While it's important to acknowledge and validate your feelings of anger, it's also crucial to find healthy ways to manage this emotion. Acting out in anger can lead to destructive behavior that you may later regret, or keeping your anger inside can manifest in your mind and body. Instead, try to find healthy outlets for your anger. Techniques to deal with anger include:

- **Acknowledge Your Feelings.** The first step in dealing with anger is to allow yourself to feel it. Don't suppress or deny your feelings. Instead, you should acknowledge them and recognize that they are normal in the grieving process. It's okay to be angry. However, you need to remember that anger is a secondary emotion because feelings of pain and hurt are usually underneath it. Allow yourself to feel these emotions, but don't let them control you. It's important to acknowledge sadness, hurt, pain, or anger when going through an emotional breakup or divorce. Acknowledging your feelings is the first step in the healing process. If these feelings are suppressed, then the grieving process will be delayed. When you are aware of your thoughts, feelings, and behaviors, you can identify patterns of behavior that may be holding you back or causing you pain.

I spent numerous weeks in tears. At times, I had deep sadness; other times, I experienced disbelief or anger. I went through various stages of grief and learned there is no right or wrong way to grieve, and there is no average length of time in which grieving should occur. Everyone is different, with different degrees of pain and hurt.

You have to remember that you must not get stuck in your grief. You have to move through it to get to the place of acceptance. You will have triggers even when you have moved through the stages. Triggers are little reminders of the pain and hurt you experienced in the past. Always remember to acknowledge all your feelings to experience healing successfully.

- **Communicate Your Feelings.** One way to release pent-up anger is to express your feelings in a healthy way. You can do this through journaling or talking to a friend. It takes courage to express your pain and hurt to someone you trust. Communicating your feelings will help to release the pain you are feeling inside. If your anger is out of control, professional support from a counselor may help you heal.

- **Think before You Act.** When you're angry, it's easy to act impulsively and say or do things you might regret later. Practicing mindfulness by taking deep breaths and being present will help you resist the urge to react impulsively. When you think before you act, you're using your brain's pre-frontal cortex, called the "thinking brain," to help process how to think and to identify healthy ways to handle your anger. Staying present keeps you from dwelling on past hurts and worrying about what will happen in the future. You will learn the importance of taking one day at a time, and even one minute or one second at a time.

Stage 3: Bargaining

Bargaining is a stage in which you try to find ways to negotiate a different outcome. You try to make deals with your ex-partner, hoping to save the relationship or find some form of closure. This stage can be especially challenging because it's an obvious sign that you're struggling to let go of the past and accept that the relationship is over.

During this stage, you may feel that you're going back and forth between wanting to reconcile and wanting to move on. It's important to remember that this is normal when you experience the loss of someone significant in your life. It's also crucial to remember that bargaining can often lead to more pain or disappointment, and it can sometimes mean that you're still having feelings of denial and not ready to accept the reality of the situation.

For example, when I discovered that my ex-husband left out crucial information about his past relationship before we got married, I bargained with him by letting him know that I would still marry him if he promised not to lie to me again. It never occurred to me that never lying again was my expectation and not his. My expectations, in hindsight, were not realistic.

If you're trying to make deals with your former partner, it's important to be realistic about your expectations. Remember that your ex-partner may not be interested in reconciling or may not be in a position to change for the sake of the relationship. It's essential to respect his or her wishes and understand their inability to want to change.

To navigate this stage, taking a step back and assessing the situation can be helpful. Ask yourself if there is anything you can realistically do to change the outcome or if you are trying to hold on to something that no longer exists. After assessing the situation, you should also set healthy boundaries. For example, if you constantly reach out to your ex-partner or engage in self-negotiation, set healthy boundaries for yourself. This might mean limiting your interactions with your ex-partner or opting for absolutely no contact, especially if the relationship is abusive. If children are involved and you must co-parent, set healthy boundaries so you can successfully move forward with your life.

Stage 4: Depression

Depression is a feeling of sadness and hopelessness. It can be incredibly challenging after a breakup or divorce because it can make you feel isolated and alone. You may feel as if no one understands what you're going through. You may feel that you're in a fog or that nothing matters anymore. Depression is a stage of grief often experienced when a relationship ends. When you experience a significant loss, such as the end of a relationship, it's normal to feel a sense of emptiness, hopelessness, and despair.

While everyone's experience of depression may differ, specific symptoms are commonly associated with this stage of grief. In addition to typical symptoms such as sadness and hopelessness, you may also find that you are emotionally and physically exhausted and that you lack energy. In addition, you might realize that your thoughts are dominated by negative feelings about yourself and your future. I experienced intense sadness in which I cried almost every day for one year. I didn't know when I would experience joy again.

One of the challenges of dealing with depression is that it can be difficult to recognize when it is happening. It is normal to feel sad and withdrawn after a breakup or divorce, but when these feelings persist for an extended period and begin to interfere with your daily life, it may be a sign that depression has set in. One of the most important things to remember when going through post-breakup depression is that it's okay to feel sad and grieve the loss of your relationship. It's a normal part of the healing process, and it's essential to allow yourself to feel your emotions and work through them in a healthy manner. During the grieving process, it is vital to take care of yourself physically. Depression can take a toll on your body, and it's essential to eat nutritious meals, get enough sleep, and exercise regularly. Taking care of yourself can help boost your mood and give you the energy you need to get through each day.

Also, exercising could help to keep your mind off the breakup. Instead of dwelling on what you cannot change, it's important to focus on the positive areas of your life and set goals for your future. This may mean pursuing a new hobby, volunteering, or taking a class. As you pursue new interests, remember that it should not replace acknowledging your feelings and working through your pain. However, focusing on things that bring you joy will help instill a sense of purpose to help you rebuild your life and find happiness again.

Stage 5: Acceptance

Acceptance is the last stage and is where you will find peace. It is a crucial part of the healing process. The time-frame to reach acceptance varies, but wounds can heal with time and with intentionally doing the necessary work. You must remember that this is not about forgetting your past relationship or dismissing your emotions; it's about acknowledging what has happened and finding a way to move forward.

During this stage, you will have scars and maybe even lingering hurt, but you'll begin to accept that the relationship is truly over. You will start to let go of the hope of a return to what used to be and to recognize that it's time to create a new chapter or season in your life. You may also better understand why the relationship ended and to learn life's lessons.

Even though acceptance is the final stage of healing, remember that it may not be a linear process to get there but a lifetime one. You may still be triggered when you are reminded of the relationship or when you meet someone new.

Most people move back and forth through the different stages before reaching acceptance. You may feel happiness and contentment one day and be overwhelmed by sadness or anger the next. Grief is a complex and evolving experience. It is essential to allow yourself the space to process your emotions and heal. When a relationship breaks up, you must grieve the dream of the "happily ever after" or "'til death do us part" vows. There is also the grief of letting go of the familiar to move to the unknown. Learning how to move through grief and processing the pain will move you to acceptance and, ultimately, healing.

I had to learn to accept that my marriage was over. The dream of growing old with my partner had died. Looking back, I learned many lessons that helped me grow, which contributed to my ability to help others find healing through their broken relationships. In the next section of this book, we will explore the healing process.

Part III

The Journey of Healing

Tune In to Your Emotions

I MENTIONED IN the previous chapter that anger is one of the stages of grief and that underneath it is hurt and pain. When you experience a relationship breakup, you must acknowledge that you are emotionally hurting. Being able to tune in to your feelings and to understand the root of what you are experiencing is essential for change to occur. Regardless of how strong you may be, your brain is wired to escape pain, so it's easy to fall into the trap of pushing your emotions aside and ignoring them, hoping they will go away. However, unexpressed emotions can build up over time and manifest in unhealthy ways. It's important to remember that healing requires that you acknowledge and process your emotions. For example, if you have been deeply hurt by someone you trusted, you must tune in to your emotions so you can heal. One way to do this is to take the time to be still, to sit quietly and see what feelings will come flooding in.

I remember staying busy when I was in pain. I needed to work as a single mother after my separation, and I thought I had to support my clients who were struggling with their mental health. I had very little time to sit still and tune in to my feelings. Since I was diagnosed with breast cancer about six months after my separation, I had little time to process my emotions. I remember finally taking the time to be still and meditate. I instantly felt the excruciating pain of sadness, hurt, loneliness, fear, and anger. I couldn't understand why my life had taken such a turn. I was angry that the person I trusted had emotionally abandoned me to deal with life's stressors. I had to acknowledge this deep pain and realize I couldn't escape it. Once I acknowledged my pain, I was on the way to healing. I learned the importance of taking the time to sit quietly to explore my feelings.

Tuning in to your emotions will help you to navigate what you are feeling and will give you a way to communicate your needs and desires to your friends and loved ones. Showing your emotions is not a weakness but a sign of strength. It's okay to feel sad, angry, and hurt. It's also okay to cry, scream if needed, or sit with your feelings. It may be uncomfortable at first, but allowing yourself to feel your emotions will help you to move through them and eventually heal.

Set Boundaries

Setting boundaries is an important step in the healing journey. After a breakup or divorce, it's important to set boundaries to protect your emotional well-being. Determining the type of relationship you will have with your ex-partner will help you to move forward with your life. If you still have romantic feelings toward your ex-partner, this may cause confusion without clear boundaries. Setting boundaries can help you feel more in control of your life and reduce stress. It will also help you create the space for new friendships and experiences when you prioritize your emotional well-being.

Create New Routines

When your relationship ends, it's important to establish new routines to get you through each day. For example, suppose you were going to specific restaurants or entertainment venues with your ex-partner or did specific activities together. In that case, it's best to find different activities or hobbies if you are still struggling due to the breakup. Your new routine can be with friends or by yourself. For example, I struggled with my birthdays because I used to have a week of celebration with my ex-husband. To help in my healing journey, I decided to pamper myself on my birthdays with massages or facials to celebrate myself rather than wait for someone else to celebrate me. Creating new routines can help you find yourself again if you have been exhausted from being in a difficult relationship. Routines can also empower and give you a sense of control over your life.

Practice Self-Care

Caring for your mind, body, and spirit will be essential in the healing journey. Self-care techniques include getting adequate hours of sleep each night, exercising several times per week, eating balanced meals daily, engaging in hobbies and activities that bring joy, spending time with friends and loved ones, and practicing mindfulness daily. Finding time to care for yourself when you have a busy schedule may seem daunting. It's easy to prioritize work, children, and other responsibilities rather than take care of yourself.

Finding the time to care for yourself is imperative because it will help speed up your recovery process. Since anxiety and depression often increase when you have experienced a traumatic relationship loss, being mindful in practicing these self-care techniques will help reduce the stress and take your mind off your pain. Studies have shown that exercising regularly will boost your mood and lower your depression as your body releases endorphins to reduce your perception of pain. Self-care demonstrates love for yourself, and it creates peace and harmony within. The Bible says that your body is God's temple, and you should take care of it. You must learn to get rid of guilt by carving out the time to care for yourself and prioritizing your self-worth.

Set Personal Goals

Setting personal goals can provide direction and allow you to rediscover the passions you had before you were in a relationship. These goals can be small ones, such as taking the time to unwind with friends once a week, or big ones, such as a career change.

I decided to return to school to complete a doctoral degree. This became important to me after my breakup and a goal that I never thought I would desire. When I completed my degree, I had a sense of pride in my accomplishment. In addition, I set a goal of buying my own home after my divorce, and the day I received the key to enter my home, I had a heart of gratitude and pride.

Goal setting can provide a sense of purpose and direction when everything around you seems bleak. It also helps reduce anxiety and stress when working toward something important to you. When you have achieved something you can be proud of, it will help restore your self-esteem and self-confidence so that you can move forward with new hope and faith to embrace this new chapter of your life with confidence.

If you are wondering how to set goals for yourself, I recommend using SMART goals. The acronym SMART means S-specific, M-measurable, A-attainable, R-realistic, and T-Time sensitive. You should write down your goals and keep them visible so you will be motivated and focused. Here is a description of the SMART goal acronym:

- **Specific**. Starting with specific and well-defined goals is essential for them to be achievable. It will clarify whether or not you have achieved them. The goals should be small enough for you to attain. An example of a goal is physically caring for yourself after a relationship breakup, and an example of a specific goal is attending two yoga classes weekly.

- **Measurable**. Goals must also be measurable, as in the example of taking two yoga classes for an hour each week. You can easily measure whether or not you attended the yoga class for one hour twice a week. If you cannot measure your identified goal to determine if it was accomplished, then you need to modify it so you can.

- **Attainable**. Goals must be attainable. If you set a goal to go to the gym every evening, but you have commitments with work or family three evenings of the week, then this goal may not be attainable. Examining your daily routines and obligations is extremely important to determine if your goals are achievable. Again, establishing small goals are more achievable than big, lofty ones.

- **Realistic**. Similar to setting goals that are attainable, it's also important that they are realistic. For example, if you'd like to try skydiving but are afraid of heights, this goal may not be realistic for you. It doesn't mean you will not be able to accomplish it; however, you may need some support in reducing your fear of heights before attempting it. You should set goals that are challenging but also achievable. It's essential to be realistic about what you can accomplish in your timeframe.

- **Time Sensitive.** Remember that goals should be time sensitive. In the example of attending yoga classes for one hour twice per week, you should also specify that it will begin today, tomorrow, next week, or next month. This will motivate you to start your goal and to evaluate if you are accomplishing it effectively.

Seek Professional Help

Emotional healing can be complex and challenging without a professional counselor's help. I have counseled numerous individuals with high anxiety and increased depression due to the trauma they experienced when their relationships ended. They realize that they are not able to get better on their own and need professional support to help them process their pain.

If you are struggling to cope with your feelings or are experiencing symptoms of depression or anxiety, a counselor you connect with can greatly support you. Therapy can provide the insight you need to become emotionally unstuck. It can also help you to find healthy coping strategies when you are not practicing good ones. The therapeutic relationship can also provide a safe place to explore your feelings, learn from your mistakes, identify your needs, and develop a plan of action to move forward to make informed choices in choosing future relationships.

For example, as a therapist, I found seeking out support after my breakup helpful. Unfortunately, I did not connect with the counselor I initially met, so I reached out to a spiritual coach who provided the insight I needed to work through my feelings and process my pain.

Learn from the Experience

A breakup or divorce can be an opportunity for internal growth and self-discovery. I learned in my couples training that "conflict is growth waiting to happen." We know that going through conflict and suffering does not feel good. We feel happy when we are in a season of reaping. However, if God created us to go through life without conflict, we would not emotionally grow or even learn to trust Him with our lives because there would be no need for that.

My relationship struggle caused me to rely on God to help me through it. A favorite scripture in Proverbs 3:5–6 states, "Trust in the Lord with all your heart; do not depend on your understanding. Seek His will in all you do, and He will show you which path to take." I had to learn to trust God and rely on trusted family members and a spiritual coach to provide support. I realized that I could not make it through my struggles alone. I learned to use my struggle to focus on personal growth and self-development.

Once you've taken the time to evaluate your relationship and identify what went wrong, it's time to identify areas of personal growth. These areas may include how to be more effective in communication, how to set good boundaries, or how to address unresolved wounds from previous relationships. During your time of reflection, you can identify valuable life lessons that help you grow as a person.

Connect with God

Connecting with God will help to release the pain you are holding on to. Expressing your thoughts and feelings in prayer will bring a great relief in knowing that you are not alone. Connecting to God reminds you that He will not leave you alone to experience this challenging season.

I had to work on being more mindful to reduce my anxiety levels. Learning to stay present and not worrying about the future made a difference. I engaged in daily prayers and devotion to get through the rough days. I prayed for God's strength and provision in my life. I also read the Bible to find encouragement, especially in times of deep sadness. One of my favorite scriptures is Philippians 4:6: "Do not be anxious about anything, but in every situation, by prayer and petition, with thanksgiving, present your requests to God." I was rarely thankful back then for the situation I was in. Instead, I was often angry about it. But I learned to release my anxiety when I prayed and stayed connected to God. Every prayer I offered to Him increased my faith and reminded me that I was not alone.

Knowing that God controls your life provides reassurance that there is still hope for the future.

Spend Time with Loved Ones

Deciding not to isolate and spending time with loved ones will help in the healing process. If you have children, taking the time to engage in play with them is very healing and causes you to stay present. Petting dogs or cats is often therapeutic because they respond with love and affection. Learning how to have fun again with loved ones and allowing them to support you will help you cope more effectively and heal more quickly. It reminds you that you are not alone.

I learned the importance of having a small core group of family members who could support me through a difficult season. I realized the importance of not going through my breakup alone.

It's so important to find close family and friends with whom you can share your emotions without feeling judged. They can help carry the load with a listening ear, words of encouragement, and a shoulder to cry on. You need to express your feelings and have someone listen without providing advice on how the situation should be handled. It would be best if you also had people who could instill hope. If you don't feel comfortable talking to those close to you, consider seeing a therapist or a coach to have a safe environment where you can share all your pain without being afraid to share your feelings.

Take One Day at a Time

You might focus on where you need to be in a particular timeframe rather than appreciating each milestone you accomplish on your way to a goal. When you are hurting, you want the pain to end when you think it's time for it to stop. Healing emotional wounds is tricky and does not happen overnight. When you carry around unresolved emotional pain, it can lead to chronic stress and anxiety. Learning to take one day at a time allows you to release the pain, which can help reduce stress. When you feel less anxious, you can better focus on the present moment and enjoy your life.

Allowing yourself to appreciate every day you get up and accomplish a task, regardless of how big or small, should be celebrated. Learning to take one day at a time and focus on the present keeps you from becoming too overwhelmed.

Serve Others

The last area of discussion is to get the focus off yourself and on to helping others. Healing occurs when you find the time to support others and make an impact, even when you are still struggling. It also helps you to realize that you are not struggling alone. Serving others will allow you to see their humanity and help them through their pain as you work on healing your own. For example, I have had numerous opportunities to support women who have struggled with traumatic relationship breakups. I have helped them to gain insight and to make decisions about how to heal and live again. Assisting others in their healing journeys and watching them experience joy again have contributed to my own healing.

Forgive Yourself

I had beaten myself up for a couple of years, asking, "How could I have missed the red flags?" I also asked God, "Why did You allow me to experience the loss of a relationship that I thought would last forever?" Although I prayed and cried and let go of my anger toward God for allowing this to happen, I continued to remind myself that I didn't do my part in opening my eyes to the truth of my relationship. I walked around with blinders and missed the warning signs needed to decipher the truth. I had a difficult time forgiving myself for trusting blindly. Although I know that trust in a relationship is normal, I realized I should have asked more questions and been more aware that my marriage was far from perfect. I had to learn to forgive my humanity and then ask God to restore my joy and help me to release self-blame.

The song "Jireh," by Elevation Worship and Maverick City Music, tells us that God is our provider and reminds us that we should be content in every circumstance that we experience. We can't change what has happened in the past, but we can be assured that God will help us to get through any situation we find ourselves in.

Forgiving yourself means that you are willing to accept what happened and you are willing to move past the mistakes to move forward with your life. Unfortunately, whatever the traumatic event, it can leave you with internal wounds, which often contribute to feelings of blame, shame, and guilt. Whatever the reason, it's imperative that you let go of self-blame, shame, and guilt because when you hold onto them, you become entangled and you are prevented from being free. It won't be easy to love again, trust again, and experience life fully if the negative feelings are not released.

Accepting your role in the relationship failure and accepting that you have to release the past, which can no longer be changed, will help free you from self-blame, shame, and guilt. It is not about downplaying what has happened but acknowledging your humanity. In an article titled "How to Forgive Yourself," author Kendra Cherry states that to forgive yourself, you should do the following:

- **Understand your emotions.** Identifying and labeling your feelings is a concept discussed earlier and a component of self-forgiveness. In fact, labeling your feelings helps to regulate guilt and shame.

- **Accept responsibility for what happened.** When you can accept responsibility, it means that you have taken the time to self-reflect and to see your role in the demise of the relationship. You also no longer will rationalize or justify your actions in the relationship.

- **Treat yourself with kindness and compassion.** As you work on forgiving yourself for your part in the breakup, it's essential to show yourself kindness and compassion. Refrain from being self-critical; instead, express love to yourself. Treat yourself in the manner that you hope others will express love to you.

- **Express remorse for your mistakes.** Remember that even if your spouse or partner wronged you,

you still have to look at your role in the relation-ship. Did you ignore the red flags? Did you stay longer than you should? Whatever your role, you must identify how you contributed to the rela-tionship breakup and express remorse so that you won't repeat the same mistakes.

- **Make amends and apologize to yourself.** Taking action to rectify the behavior is a way to make amends to yourself. When you realize the benefit of knowing that you did the best that you could based on your situation, it will allow you to let go of self-blame and to forgive yourself.

- **Look for ways to learn from the experience.** Remember that in every situation you find your-self in; a lesson needs to be learned. Even when your experience is traumatic, you can learn about yourself and your circumstance. Every mistake or failure is an opportunity for self-awareness and emotional growth.

- **Focus on making better choices in the future.** Understanding your role in the breakup will help you learn from your mistakes and provide insight into making better decisions in the future. This knowledge will guide your future decision-making.

Forgiveness and Boundary Setting with Ex-Partner

Being hurt by someone you love and trust can be heartbreaking and difficult to forgive. Forgiveness is important because it helps free you from lingering hurt and anger. It allows you to let go of the other person's wrongs and forgive yourself for your decisions. Many people think that when you have forgiven someone who has hurt you, you must reconcile with him or her. However, if you remain in a relationship with someone who continues to hurt and abuse you, you are choosing to give that person an opportunity to hurt you again. Understanding that you can forgive and still set boundaries so that you will no longer be a victim is a healthy way to heal.

The Lord's Prayer declares that we should forgive those who trespass against us. This is often difficult to do when your heart is broken. When hurting, you may resort to a "flight, fight, or freeze" response to protect yourself. You will naturally go through a grieving period and probably lose sight of your desires and goals for a period of time. You experience disbelief that your situation is happening to you and is out of your control. You may experience anger and resentment toward the person who caused the pain. At times you may desire to bargain with the person or yourself to regain control of your life. You may also experience depression, worry, and loneliness when you face loss. At some point, you need to get to the place of acceptance of the loss so that you can successfully move forward in your life rather than remaining stuck.

I counseled Shelly, who was being physically abused by her boyfriend. He would express remorse whenever he abused her. She would forgive him and remain in the relationship until she was beaten again. She was finally able to leave him and work on forgiving him and herself for not leaving earlier than she did. She was able to set boundaries with him so that she could be emotionally free, even though they had a child together.

Paula also left her spouse after seven years of marriage. She discovered he cheated and had a child with his mistress during their marriage. Paula was devastated that her husband was unfaithful, especially since this was her second marriage. Although he was remorseful and wanted her to forgive him and salvage the marriage, she decided it was time to move on with her life. She finally let go of the marriage so she could heal. Paula could forgive him and stay in touch as friends when she finally moved on. They were able to have an amicable divorce and to check in on each other as needed. After her divorce, Paula opened her heart to love again, and she met a man she later married. She could give and receive love in her new relationship by forgiving her ex-husband and establishing boundaries with him.

When my marriage came crashing down, I mourned the loss. I was hurt, so I naturally retreated. But unfortunately, my hurt turned into anger, so I had to go through the stages of grief. I realized that I had to do the work of forgiveness so I would not remain stuck. Forgiveness is a challenging process. I learned that it's not enough to say, "I forgive you." The deeds or behaviors must follow. I needed to remember that we all enter relationships with the baggage we carry from childhood, trying to get our wounds healed.

Rather than looking within to identify your wounds and work on your healing, you might look to others to fill the emptiness. Consequently, the healing occurs from within, not from the outside. As a fallen human being, you might unintentionally hurt those closest to you. You learn that when someone hurts you, it's more about that person's brokenness. You can rise above the pain when you see the bigger picture so that forgiveness becomes more attainable. Remember that forgiveness doesn't mean you must stay in an unhealthy relationship. You have to go deep within and examine and reexamine your life.

You have to determine what is true for you. My truth was to move forward and still have compassion for the man I shared my heart and life with for many years. I realized that it's okay to set boundaries for myself to heal. I needed time and space to work through the pain his brokenness had created in my life. I needed to work through the triggers that reminded me of my disappointment in my ex-husband for being dishonest. I had to tell someone I loved, "Enough! I can't do it anymore," so I could fully grieve. I learned that I had to let go of judgment so I could forgive. I realized that I needed to pray for him so God would release anger from my spirit.

I also had to show my child that I could co-parent with her father even though we were no longer together. Learning how to co-parent effectively has been a significant factor in our lives and has been healthy for all of us. I had to learn that forgiveness is a continual act, especially when I was triggered. Forgiveness has allowed me to be free on the inside so I can move forward with my life. It also allows me to sincerely wish the best for the man who has caused so much pain in my life.

When we can have compassion for those who trespass against us, we set our hearts free. This is how we practice forgiveness.

Whenever you feel anger inside, take the time to examine what you are experiencing. God created all of your emotions, but you are to take control of them rather than let them control you. God's Word discusses the importance of not allowing anger to become a sin. His Word also says not to let it fester within your heart; you have to release it. You release it when you can forgive yourself for what you did, should have done, or didn't do. You release it when you do not let someone else's behavior take away your joy and passion for living. You release anger when your behavior demonstrates that you can show kindness, even to the person who has caused the hurt. Forgiveness is achievable and needed to experience inner peace and freedom.

A great example of forgiveness is found in Scripture in the book of Genesis. Joseph was the youngest of twelve brothers. He was sold into slavery by his brothers due to jealousy. Even though Joseph experienced great adversity when he was betrayed, he persevered through his challenges until he was elevated to leadership. Unfortunately, in another incident, Joseph stayed true to his values but was punished for something he did not do and went to prison. He learned the importance of finding his purpose while he was imprisoned and continued to have hope despite his circumstances. When Joseph was finally released from prison, he was elevated to a place of authority under the country's ruler. He used his platform to examine the present and understand God's plan for the future. He was scarred from his past, but he did not let his experiences hinder him from following God's direction to prepare for the future and release the pain of the past. When his brothers arrived in Israel, they did not recognize him.

Joseph was able to be generous to his brothers because of his ability to forgive them for hurting him. He realized that although his brothers rejected and abandoned him, God used the brokenness he experienced to fulfill his purpose. Joseph helped not only his brothers but also an entire nation during times of crisis. He learned the importance of releasing all bitterness so he could heal within. He realized that forgiveness was important to free himself to move forward with his life. Joseph did that and received abundant blessings after tremendous loss.

This biblical story is a reminder that even when you experience adversity, you can still find your purpose. The pain of a betrayal can be devastating, but it does not have to be the end of your story. Turning the pain into purpose gives hope. Learning to forgive will free you from being imprisoned mentally and emotionally since it allows you to open your heart to love again.

Part IV

A Season of Awakening

A SEASON OF awakening is when you reflect on your experiences, even when they are traumatic, and grow from them. You decide to take control of your life and become intentional to manifest the outcome you desire personally and in your next relationship. Researchers Kansky and Allen found that there are more studies done on the distress that occurs after a relationship breakup than the potential for growth that it brings. Although a romantic breakup is a traumatic experience for many people, they determined that individuals can bounce back with a higher level of functioning and well-being, called post-traumatic growth. They found that individuals can gain better conflict management and communication skills, contributing to more emotional stability, increased self-growth, and greater overall satisfaction in future romantic relationships. Therefore, when a traumatic season ends, you can learn from the experience and take the lessons learned to embrace a new chapter of your life. Taking the time to understand your past will inform and shape your future. Let's explore how to experience an awakening after a breakup to reclaim your inner peace and joy.

The Wilderness Experience

Everyone experiences the wilderness season, which is a time of intense suffering and pain. You feel alone and broken. Learning how to make it through the wilderness season can be difficult when all you see are trees. This is when you turn to God and believe He will take us out of the wilderness experience.

This reminds me of the Israelites who wandered in the wilderness for forty years, hoping to get to the Promised Land. The people who made it there were those who were obedient to God's teachings. When you are disobedient to what God is telling you to do, you may find yourself going around in circles, trying to find your way, just as the Israelites did.

Being in a wrong relationship can feel as if you are in the wilderness experience. It can cause sadness or anxiety when the relationship does not align with what God has for you.

I know when I am not in alignment. When I enter into a relationship because I feel lonely, even though I know within my spirit that this is not the person God has chosen for me, I am telling God that I do not trust Him to be my provider.

You do not want to be in a wilderness experience—no one does—but it is where you grow the most. You learn you can't rely on your strength to get through it. You have to depend on God and His timing for the partner He will bring into your life. Waiting can be difficult when you are in the wilderness season. However, Scripture says, "We should not be weary in well doing, for in due time we shall reap" (Galatians 6:9). When the wrong relationship has ended and you are waiting for God to send the right one, you need to remain steadfast in your faith while you wait for the right person to come along.

Mindset Shift

One thing you have to remember is not to limit yourself. When your experiences are complex, you must learn to lean into the struggle and not run away from it. You also learn what you are capable of accomplishing through your struggle. You learn to grow through your pain. After you have grieved your loss, you have to take the time to focus on the message you give yourself. You have to remember your worth despite the relationship breakup. You must remember the lessons from the broken relationship in which you can learn and grow. If you find yourself struggling with depression or anxiety, take the time to address them before they get out of control.

You should first acknowledge your thoughts and how they affect your emotions and behavior to be able to change your mindset. If you are experiencing negative thoughts about your breakup or struggling with negative thoughts about yourself, you must challenge these thoughts. This means asking yourself whether or not your thoughts are reasonable. Often, what you worry about will never come to pass. Even if you experience a traumatic event, your past experiences do not dictate your future experiences if you take the time to heal. You have desires and plans that you would like to accomplish. However, you might begin to doubt that you are valuable and worthy of receiving what you desire. Instead of speaking them into existence, you might sow negative thoughts. If you sow negative doubts, you will reap a negative outcome. If you sow positive thoughts, then you can see your desires manifested.

When you acknowledge your negative thoughts, the next step is to change them to something more positive. For example, even if you experienced disappointment from a partner you trusted, you can tell yourself that you will meet someone honest and trustworthy to share your life with again. It is so important to correct your cognitive distortions to release anxiety and depression in your life. The Bible says to be transformed by renewing your mind (Romans 12:2). It takes faith to believe that the broken relationships you experienced were life lessons preparing you for something more beautiful and great. Changing the negative mindset to a positive one will propel the healing journey and allow you to have an open heart to experience the blessings God has in store for you. How do you challenge your thoughts to change your negative mindset to a positive one? Here are some techniques for doing so:

- **Release Negative Thoughts.** Picture a traffic light in front of you, and use the red light to stop your thoughts from racing. Refute negative thinking. Challenge it to see if it is accurate. If it's not, replace the negative thought with one that is true. Write down the reason why the negative thoughts continue to persist, then write the message you want to hear. Spend the next twenty-one days repeating the positive words you want to hear. Speak the desires of your heart daily. Research indicates that if we do something for twenty-one days, it becomes a habit. When you begin to visualize your desires, every fiber of your being will move in that direction.

- **Abundance Mindset.** To have an abundance mindset, you must determine the root of the scarcity mindset. Perhaps you were told growing up that you should hold on to whatever you have because you may not receive anything better. If you have internalized this belief system, you will have difficulty letting go of a bad relationship to receive the one you deserve. You have to believe that something better is waiting for you. It's about believing you are worthy to receive a relationship that's right for you because there is a potential partner also doing the work in preparing to meet you. You learn to release all the self-sabotaging thoughts that keep you stuck and welcome the abundance of self-affirmation thoughts that build you up.

- **Practice Silence.** Learn how to be still and go deep within to hear the thoughts in your head. You may move through life so quickly that you don't hear your thoughts. You may be afraid to slow down long enough because you are afraid to listen to what you are thinking. You struggle to control your thoughts; therefore, you keep busy so you don't have to address them. Taking control of your thoughts requires you to be still. When you acknowledge your thoughts, then you can work on changing them.

- **Take Deep Breaths.** When you are silent, remember not to judge your thoughts. If your thoughts become overwhelming, take a deep, cleansing breath from your diaphragm. Doing so allows the brain to calm down and slow your racing thoughts, and it's easier to think more rationally with less fear. Deep breaths will enable you to release any lingering stress in your body and to calm down. It increases your energy and mindfulness so you will gain clarity about when to move forward or to remain still. It also brings insight into the steps you should take in a relationship. Take the time to breathe and slow down so you will know how to move forward.

- **Know Your Worth.** In "Shine Bright like a Diamond," Rihanna sings, "I choose to be happy … You and I … We're like diamonds in the sky." You should allow your light to shine, as the Bible says. However, you have to know your worth to have your light shine brightly. How often has your light dimmed because you are in an unfulfilled and broken relationship? How many times have you forgotten your worth and allowed someone else to define your worth for you? Knowing your worth or value is showing with confidence that you are significant. You love and accept who you are and don't need someone else to tell you that you are worthy to believe it. When you genuinely understand your value, you will wait for God's promise instead of settling for crumbs because you can't wait for His timing. How often have you settled for someone who takes you off your purpose? How often have you given your heart to someone who cannot truly love and protect you? It's time to end this behavior and allow God's timing to dominate your existence. It's time to let your internal light shine.

Fulfilling Your Purpose

It's important to know what you are called to do in the waiting season and to do it. Knowing your purpose and fulfilling it are critical to experiencing joy. Sometimes you might focus on finding a partner rather than doing what you are called to do. When you fulfill your purpose, you become less focused on what you don't have in your life.

I remember feeling sorry for myself. At times, I felt alone and disillusioned. I would ask God, "Why must I do everything alone? Why can't I experience love? Will I become too old to find love again? Why is it so hard to find my perfect match?" The more I thought about not having someone special in my life, the more depressed and anxious I became. I knew I had to change my negative thinking. I knew I had to trust that God had a plan more incredible than I could imagine as I did the work He called me to do. I realized that the worry of being alone kept me from fully surrendering to God's will and purpose for my life. I learned that a partner could show up when I least expected it as I focused on fulfilling my purpose. God gave me a vision to write this book, to support more couples, and to train other therapists to get back on track to continue to fulfill my purpose on this earth. In the same way, when you focus on fulfilling God's calling, you will begin to trust that He will bring your partner in His perfect time.

Waiting Patiently

Patience is one of the fruits of the spirit listed in the Bible. Scripture identifies love, joy, peace, patience, kindness, generosity, faithfulness, gentleness, and self-control as the areas we should develop to be spiritually strengthened. Patience in the waiting season can be challenging. This is an area that I continually have to cultivate in my life.

The Israelites had to wander in the desert for forty years when they left Egypt because they lacked patience and faith that God would bring them to the Promised Land. Even though they saw God's miracles, such as the parting of the Red Sea and the provision of daily manna from heaven for their sustenance, they still doubted that they would see God's promise because it took too long. Their lack of patience caused them to make decisions outside of God's will. They made graven objects to worship and rejected God when their prayers were not answered immediately. Their lack of patience caused them to go around in circles. Even though they could have reached the Promised Land within a few months, God allowed them to wander for forty years instead. Due to their disobedience, most of the Israelites died and did not receive the promise.

How many times have you gone to God with a request? You may say that you believe He will answer your prayers, but when it doesn't happen right away, you begin to doubt His promise to you. Sometimes you may decide that God is taking too long, so you might settle for someone who appears to fit the relationship you want and compromise on some fundamental core values. When you compromise and do not wait for God's perfect timing, you could set yourself up for a relationship filled with insurmountable conflict. Waiting patiently can be difficult; however, not waiting patiently can bring about undue stress, possibly contributing to a life filled with regrets.

Embracing Singleness

Embracing singleness can be scary if you have been married or have been in a long-term relationship for an extended period. However, learning to be content with whatever state you are in is a biblical concept. It doesn't mean you don't want to be married again or to be in another committed relationship; it just means that you need to be in a place where you are happy, are accepting your singleness, and are whole. You may be afraid to be alone, but you must learn to experience solitude and to be content before you can appreciate being in partnership with someone else. It can be tempting to jump into a new relationship right after a breakup or divorce to cope with any lingering hurt you may be experiencing. If you have just ended a relationship and are working on healing, you should not set a goal of finding a healthy relationship right away. Although you may be able to find a new partner, the relationship may not be beneficial. Rushing into a new relationship before you're emotionally ready can lead to more heartache and can make it harder for you to move on.

Taking the time to participate in activities on your own that help you grow is a critical step in the healing journey. For example, sitting in a restaurant alone and not worrying that something is wrong with you is a good growth experience. It's okay to attend events without a partner if there is an activity that you would like to participate in.

I attended an international conference on my own, even though spouses or partners were invited to attend. I enjoyed the serenity of the beach and the solitude of tuning in to my thoughts and feelings. I enjoyed making decisions without having to check in with a partner. Many times I felt I would have enjoyed these experiences with a partner; however, I realized that I needed to value the adventure I was experiencing by myself. I learned to be grateful for each day and to release worrying about tomorrow.

Part V

A Season of Hope

Assess Your Relationship Readiness

Knowing when you are ready for love is an interesting question. Just because you are single again does not mean you are ready for love. Even if you think you are ready, it does not necessarily mean that you are. Resist the urge to focus on meeting a new partner due to feelings of loneliness. It is difficult to process your feelings when you are feeling lonely. Doing the work to heal the pain of a breakup is a crucial step in being able to love again. You can't rush the healing process. You may need several months or even several years. It's less about the time and more about the work needed to process the pain of the breakup. Acknowledging your feelings and learning from past experiences are critical in moving forward. Being able to ask the question, "What is the lesson in my pain?" will help bring clarity. Understanding how both you and your ex-partner contributed to the relationship breakup is another important step. When the work is done, you will experience inner peace.

You will know when you are ready to be vulnerable again. You will know when you desire to give your love and receive it in return. You will be able to attract someone who has also done the work and to have the discernment to release someone from your life who is not ready to love. Being prepared to love again is an experience of "knowing." You will desire to truly connect emotionally, spiritually, and physically with a partner. It's an indescribable feeling of yearning. When you get to that place, you will know it's time.

Opening Your Heart

How do you open your heart again to trust fully? I often asked myself this question after being deeply hurt in my previous relationship. I wasn't sure if I could return to a place of vulnerability to love again after being in a dark place where I was hurt. I remember getting through my days by keeping busy to avoid the pain. I remember feeling despair. I had lost my best friend and lover. However, after several years of doing the work to address the trauma, I finally wanted to open my heart to love again.

I have seen many people hold on to the anger and bitterness that can quickly appear from being hurt. As a therapist, I realized that all the things that I learned were put to the test in my own situation. I had to learn how to rise above the pain and release my anger so it would not become resentment. I had to let go of bitterness to move on with my life. I realized that the lessons I taught had to manifest in my own life. I had to let go of the fear of loving again and find ways to live my life fully. If I didn't do this, everything I taught my clients would be false. Everything I believed would become null and void. Holding on to my hurt is the same as saying that I am a victim and my life is hopeless. I decided that this would not be the trajectory of my life. No one was going to stop me from living whole. I had to find a way to heal so my heart would love again.

If you have been hurt by someone you love, you will feel angry. But happier days are around the corner. I don't know when it will come, but it will. A storm in your life hurts the most when you have given so much of yourself to someone else. It's like losing a part of yourself. Sometimes you may feel empty on the inside. Other times, you may feel as if a part of you died. But don't despair; there is hope. You may wonder how to move through the pain to experience hope and trust and eventually learn to love again. Here are a few steps to help you in this process, which are essential steps to healing.

Surrendering Your Will

Surrendering your will and releasing it to God means acknowledging that you are not in control of your life, but the Creator is in complete control. It doesn't mean that you give up. However, it does mean that you ask God for your desires to align with His will. It takes a great deal of surrender to have a posture of humility. It's difficult to release control and surrender to God, even if you understand His power to direct your life. In the process of surrender, you cease striving to make a relationship happen. You do the work to heal and open your heart to allow God to guide your path. When you are in the place of surrender, you continue to live life to the fullest and accept whatever life unfolds after the work is done. You learn to release all fears and walk in faith when you have surrendered. You tell God that you are ready to accept His perfect will for your life, even if it's not what you pictured.

God's Timing

Waiting for God's timing to meet the person who should be in your life can seem daunting. It takes great faith to hold on to the vision that God will allow you to meet the person He has prepared for you. If you settle for a partner out of desperation, you will miss God's perfect plan for your life.

Many times, I was discouraged that I had to attend events alone. I experienced many successes but did not have a partner to share them with after my divorce. I often reminded myself that I should not settle for just anyone who came into my life. Sometimes I was told I was "too picky" or was not giving someone a chance to know me. I began to doubt myself, thinking I was expecting too much and afraid I might remain single forever. I had to listen to my inner voice that reminded me that I should not settle for a man with whom I didn't have a solid connection.

Learning ito wait and listen to God's voice before proceeding will help you recognize the person God has prepared for you. When both individuals feel they have met the person God has prepared for them, they experience peace. Waiting for His timing takes faith, trust, and patience.

God's timing is important to have in your life. Waiting can be challenging because God's timing is often not what you desire. It is often difficult to be in a season of waiting. It's usually not fun to wait for God to answer your prayers. When you are in the season of waiting, you give up control. You learn to rely on God and trust Him to know what is best for you. When you trust that God's timing is always right, it helps to reduce anxiety and makes you feel more secure about your future. Fear creeps in when you worry that your desires will not be manifested, and you think God has forgotten your needs. However, understanding that He knows what you need in every season of your life, will enable you to be ready to receive the person He is preparing for you.

Surrender is essential as it increases your faith and connection to God. The definition of surrender is to "yield to the power, control, or possession of another." When you take control of your life and do not yield to the Creator, you can easily miss out on what God wants for you. Learning to surrender and trust God for His timing will allow you to meet the person God has ordained for you.

It's incredibly difficult to go through the waiting season. It can be filled with anxiety, unrest, turmoil, loneliness, and fear. You must remember that the best way to get through it is to take the time to heal fully and to feel comfortable with your singleness. It's also important to examine areas of your life that need healing. Often, God is preparing the heart and mind of the prospective partner He has for you.

During the waiting season, you'll learn to be still and to listen to God's voice and to be content in your circumstances. It's learning to say "no" to someone unsuitable for you, even if you are tempted to say "yes" because you feel lonely. Isaiah 60:22 states, "No matter what you may be facing today, trust in God's assurance that everything will fall into place in His perfect time." What an amazing assurance. It's difficult to remember this when you are being tried and tested. Job 23:10 says, "When he has tried me, I shall come forth as gold." It's hard to wait and not doubt when you don't know when your hopes and dreams will be manifested. However, when you successfully trust God's timing, you shall receive your reward.

Tenfold Restoration

Restoration feels amazing after you have experienced loss. This is the process of returning something to its original condition by repairing it. In the Bible, Job experienced the loss of his family, his health, and his friends. He cried out to God in his despair. His friends thought he must have sinned, which caused him to lose almost everything. Job ignored what everyone told him and asked God to help him through his pain. He was restored tenfold due to his faithfulness. However, this restoration did not come without scars. Job received ten times his original possessions and ten more children, but he still had to endure the hurt of losing his original ten children. Although he experienced restoration, his scars were a reminder of the suffering he endured and his willingness to surrender to God's perfect plan for his life.

I truly believe God will restore your blessings and grant you favor beyond your expectations.

Have family and friends told you it's time to get out and date again, even when you're not ready? Remember, you are the only one who knows if the time is right. Remember that you must be healed to attract a new partner who is also healed. It's easy to rush the timeline due to pressure from family and friends. They might even begin to set up blind dates for you because they think a particular person is right for you. Although that person might be a good fit, it will work only if you are ready to love again. Remember to communicate your desires and set boundaries that are right for you.

Suppose your healing is complete, but you are afraid to date again because you don't want another failed relationship. It's important to believe that a failed relationship is not the end of the story. You have to be in a place of surrender to trust that God can restore what is lost. Even though your romantic relationship has ended, after healing, you can find a perfect relationship the second or even the third time around.

In a previous chapter, I mentioned Paula, who experienced two breakups when she discovered that both spouses cheated on her during her marriages. Although she experienced two failed marriages, she took the time to heal and opened her heart to fall in love again. A few years later, Paula met her third husband. She is now happily married, and they are thriving as a couple.

I believe that when God restores what has been lost, you learn not to take your blessings for granted. You appreciate the person who is in your life, and you do whatever it takes to preserve the relationship. You learn to love deeply and do so with more urgency. You begin to fully understand the importance of going through the waiting season to receive the manifestation of the blessings God has in store for you.

Release Comparisons

It's easy to get into a new relationship and compare the new person to the previous one. These comparisons may include what you believe are good or bad qualities of the person you broke up with. Maybe you liked it when your ex-partner cuddled on the couch and talked to you while you were both watching a movie, but the new partner wants to sit next to you and focus on the TV screen, not you. It's easy to begin comparing because you miss some aspects of what your ex-partner did. However, it's important to remember that your ex-partner is your ex for a reason.

It's time to focus on the new person in your life so you won't lose out on the relationship God has for you. Remember to treat him or her as an individual because that's how you want to be treated. Can you imagine how you would feel in a new relationship if you were compared to an ex-partner? It would not last because your self-esteem would be impacted. You don't want to be in a relationship in which you feel that you are second best. Remember to treat your new partner in the way you want to be treated. Accept that person as God created him or her to be, with good qualities and even flaws.

The Law of Attraction

Many books have been written about the universal law of attraction, which asserts that your thoughts and actions bring about certain outcomes. The biblical principle is that you reap what you sow. If you sow negative thoughts, doubt, and fear, you will reap them. If you change the negative self-talk and speak words of life, you will reap what you desire. This is the same for the partner you want in your life. If you express the type of relationship you want and the type of partner you desire, you will attract what you believe.

One of my clients introduced me to the book *The Soulmate Secret: Manifest the Love of Your Life with the Law of Attraction*. The author gives countless examples of people manifesting their partners because they spoke what they wanted and made provisions for them. My client made room in her closet for her soulmate as an act of faith. This demonstrated that she believed it would happen. She also wrote down the specifics of what she desired in a partner, which helped her recognize her soulmate when he arrived.

After a divorce, it's easy to doubt that a purpose partner is waiting to meet you. This is especially true when you thought your marriage would not end. Overcoming your doubt and fear so you can believe that God has someone handpicked for you is essential to the law of attraction. All doubt and fear must dissipate to manifest your desires.

My friend Cassie went through a divorce. After trying tirelessly to reconcile with her spouse, she finally decided to let him go since he was not interested in reconciling. She took a couple of years to heal and decided that she wanted to be married to a man with a strong Christian faith. She finally met Mack, who lived a few hours away from her. How did she manifest him? Well, she knew she wanted to share her life with someone who loved her and could embrace her children. She decided to meet a new partner using an online dating platform.

Cassie met some men she liked, but the relationships did not work out. She worked through her frustration by believing she would meet someone using the platform. She expressed her desires and took her request to God. After meeting a few single men unsuitable for her, she widened her search to find Mack. He was also looking for his soulmate after a failed marriage. He said he was looking for a woman with a strong Christian faith. He proposed after a few short months, and they had an intimate wedding with family and friends to celebrate their union. They are thrilled that they found each other. Cassie and Mack manifested their desires by being clear about what they wanted. They decided to move forward to a commitment quickly because they both prayed about what they desired and saw these qualities in each other.

Part VI

Preparing for a Healthy Relationship

MANY PEOPLE SEEK to enter new relationships or to remarry after a divorce. However, studies show the rate of divorce is equally high in first and second marriages. This is because many people enter into new relationships without doing the work as outlined in previous chapters. To have a new relationship, specific techniques must be followed to succeed. This section will outline the areas that should be considered for a successful relationship or marriage. Let's examine these steps closely.

Relationship Pursuit

Studies indicate that 60 percent of men initiate relationships, but 30 percent of couples report that it's equally divided between men and women. Since men are more likely to initiate relationships, we will focus on the man's pursuit of the woman. When a man is interested in a woman, he will make his intentions known by pursuing her to demonstrate his interest. No one else matters to him except the woman he desires. He makes time for a connection, and he hopes to get to know her. He wants her to know his intentions by expressing his desire to have a relationship with her.

Being in a place of vulnerability is difficult, especially if one has been previously hurt in a romantic relationship. When a man pursues a woman, he might be fearful of getting hurt if the woman rejects his advances. It may trigger hurt feelings from a past relationship and may cause him to shut down. But if he has been through the healing process, he will put aside his fears and pursue anyway. He will have an intense feeling to go after the woman who makes his heart open again. If both the man and the woman have taken the time to heal, they will be clear about what they need and desire. Communicating these needs upfront will help reduce the hurt they may fear experiencing again.

When a woman is interested in a relationship, she will be receptive to a man's pursuit. She will make her interest known by giving cues that she desires to be pursued and is interested in getting to know him. Some women do not subscribe to this traditional view and have successfully found a committed relationship when they have pursued it. Although exceptions always exist, traditional roles continue to be the norm.

Emotionally Healthy

Regardless of who pursues the relationship, it is more important for both individuals to have done the work to heal fully. Couples could shortchange themselves if both partners are not emotionally healed from past relationships. Healthy relationships can happen when both individuals have done their healing work and are ready to love again.

If a potential partner has not yet healed, you are doing yourself a disservice by pursuing a relationship with a reduced chance of succeeding. You will receive what you deserve only when you know your worth.

The Art of Communication

Communicating effectively in any relationship is essential. When people struggle with understanding and implementing good communication techniques, then relationships break down. Many couples undergo therapy due to communication breakdowns in their relationships. When there is conflict, it is easy for couples to focus on being heard rather than learning how to listen, validate, and empathize with each other. People some-times avoid working through conflicts because they experienced maladaptive communication patterns growing up. Learning proper techniques will help couples avoid lingering conflict, communicate their thoughts and feelings more effectively, and listen to each other's frustrations instead of being reactive. There are many techniques to improve communication.

Author Harville Hendrix identified one such theory in his book *Getting the Love You Want*, which discusses the importance of mirroring, validating, and expressing empathy in a relationship. Each of these will be discussed in more detail to understand how this technique can apply to couples in conflict. According to Hendrix, mirroring involves actively listening to what your partner is communicating. You have to give your partner your undivided attention and eliminate all distractions. You must learn how to suspend your thoughts while listening without trying to formulate a response. Often, couples become defensive or avoidant when they are in conflict. Learning to be present in the moment to fully understand your partner will encourage the practice of active listening.

Mirroring

Mirroring means reflecting on your partner's words and sending them back word for word, providing a summary, or paraphrasing them. Any of these methods will let your partner know he or she is being heard. Mirroring also makes both individuals feel valued and respected because they are committed to giving each other undivided time to speak and be heard. Mirroring slows down and enhances the communication process. The focus is less on solving a conflict and more on letting your partner know that what he or she has to say is important.

Here is an example of mirroring:

One person might say, "I feel frustrated when you spend hours every day scrolling through social media rather than spending time with me."

The partner might respond, "I heard you say that you are frustrated when I spend several hours each day on social media instead of spending more time with you."

When both individuals feel that they are heard, it will help improve the patterns of communication and can increase connection.

Validation

Validation is critical in helping you communicate with your partner because he or she informs you that the information mirrored makes sense. It brings assurance that your feelings are valid because your partner can see your perspective. In her article in *Psychology Today*, Karyn Hall states that validation communicates acceptance of your partner's thoughts, feelings, and understandable behaviors. It does not necessarily mean that you agree, but it lets your partner know that you support and value the relationship even though you may have a different perspective. It communicates that you can still appreciate the importance of your partner's thoughts and feelings, even in disagreement. Couples often struggle to communicate because they think it means they have to agree with each other. Hendrix states that in a relationship, there are two points of view, and each person is entitled to his or her own truth.

Couples learn to listen to each other's point of view and will increase trust and connection when one validates the other. An example of validation is when one partner has communicated a frustration, and the other responds by saying, "What makes sense about what I just heard is that you feel frustrated when I'm preoccupied with social media, and I neglect to spend time with you. You feel the lack of time spent together contributes to our disconnection." This makes the frustrated person feel that his or her feelings are making sense. Validation can be challenging; however, when you can let go of your need to be correct and focus on understanding your partner's needs, growth begins. I teach couples about the importance of learning how to do this. It's usually a challenge for most of them, but couples who thrive learn how to do this successfully.

Empathy

Empathy is another essential step in improving communication in a relationship. It is the capacity to understand and feel what another person is experiencing from his or her frame of reference. To enhance communication, both individuals must understand each other's feelings by reflecting on what is being communicated and imagining what the experience is like for the partner. To communicate empathy effectively, each person must learn to tap into his or her partner's hurt and pain. An example of empathy in a couple's dialogue after the person has communicated frustration is, "I imagine you must feel sad and alone when I don't spend time with you." This dialogue encourages an emotional connection in the relationship.

The Power of Intention to Manifest Your Desires

To manifest the type of relationship you truly desire, you must set your intentions to do so. You must believe you are worthy to receive someone the Creator has designed for you and imagine yourself connecting with that person. You also have to accept the season you are currently in and live each day with intention. When you believe that God has a plan for your life, you begin to trust that everything will work according to His plan. You will then begin to release self-doubt and fear and believe that your desires will be manifested if they are according to God's will. When you begin to have faith, you shift your mindset.

Taking Responsibility for Your Actions

How often have you experienced disappointment or hurt, and you blame other people for the mess you find yourself in? It's the same with a broken relationship. You may feel that you wouldn't be struggling with years of hurt and pain if the person you fell in love with didn't hurt you. Taking responsibility for your actions to manifest your desires means you must be introspective to determine your role in relationships. How do people see you? How do you show up in the world? What energy do you project when you are with others? What did you accept in your life that you should not have? Are you your authentic self around other people? How did you contribute to the demise of your relationship? Who did you accept in your life even though you knew the person was not right for you? These questions and many more will help you to take responsibility for your actions and prepare you to manifest your desires. This journey is necessary to heal fully. No shortcuts are allowed, or you will continue to repeat the same path until you gain the insight for change to happen to receive the type of relationship you truly want.

The Power to Choose

You were created to have free will. Regardless of your upbringing, even if you were born into poor social and economic conditions, you have the power to choose your path. You may have fewer opportunities due to injustices in our society. However, despite the circumstances you experienced in your past, you have the power to rise above them and fight for what you desire. Your journey may not be smooth, but it is possible. You must choose to be a victor and not a victim. Despite the situation you are in, you have to decide to take control and not let your circumstances prevent it. You must look at what you desire, not your current or past circumstances. You have to choose to stand in your power and not let anyone take it from you. Even when you fear that you may not be able to find a healthy relationship that you desire, remember to choose to do your inner work and only let people into your life who have done the work. You must rise above your circumstances to manifest the relationship you want.

Surrendering Your Will

It seems difficult to surrender your will and take control of your power simultaneously. However, surrendering your will means that you no longer believe that you must be in control for everything to work out the way you want. Your life is not yours alone; your existence is due to the work of the Creator. You must believe that He is in control of your life and the plans you have for the future.

Surrender is a powerful concept because it involves a high level of faith to trust that God has the best for you and knows the path you should take to remain in His will. A scripture in Proverbs reminds us that we make our plans, but the Creator directs our steps. Surrender is a decision to let go so that God can take control of your life. When you are in a place of surrender, you release fears that your life will not be okay. You begin to believe that everything will work out according to the Creator's plan, and because of this belief, you will begin to manifest the life that He has determined for you to live. You begin to listen to the still, small inner voice that tells you the steps to take to remain in His will.

Establishing Boundaries for Yourself

Setting boundaries can be difficult. This may be due to a fear of not being liked when you set boundaries with others. However, when you don't set boundaries, you invite people to take advantage of you. You are telling them that their needs are more important than yours. This is seen in all types of relationships, including romantic ones. Many relationships break down because of a fear of establishing boundaries early in the relationship. You may assume that you don't have to set boundaries because if your partner loves you, he or she should know that some things are unacceptable.

Unfortunately, the lack of communication will bring hurt and resentment. Learning to say no is critical, even if your partner does not like it. Being able to express your own needs is an important element in a healthy relationship. Communicating your boundaries takes intentionality and self-love. You must understand that having a healthy relationship means being clear about your needs and effectively communicating them to the other person. Healthy boundaries will lead to healthy relationships. It is a demonstration of self-worth.

Accepting Yourself

You are an individual with unique physical features, personality, and characteristics. Regardless of your race, gender, ethnicity, and social standing, you are made in the image of God. You are unique in God's eyes and are called to fulfill your calling on this earth. You must accept your uniqueness and love yourself, even if you feel that you are not accepted and loved by others.

Learning to accept yourself is an act of self-love. Self-acceptance means you understand you have imperfections, but despite your flaws, you accept that you are perfectly imperfect. You decide what areas you want to change without condemning yourself. Being able to affirm yourself daily helps to increase the level of love you have for yourself. You cannot manifest your true desires unless you accept yourself in every aspect. To manifest a healthy relationship, you must understand and accept both your and your partner's shortcomings. You no longer have to wait for someone else to validate you to feel good about yourself. You understand your worth because you know your value. You will manifest the relationship you want because you don't need someone else to make you feel whole.

Choosing to Soar

Knowing that you set the ceiling of what you want for yourself is a big part of manifesting your desires. Even when others have a ceiling of what you can receive in your life, it does not have to be the one you set for yourself. This applies to romantic relationships also. Although you may have experienced hurt and heartache in a past relationship, you must believe that the right person is waiting for you. You must know that you can soar beyond all the challenges you have experienced to receive the love that you desire. You must believe that the only limits you will encounter are those you set for yourself. I have chosen not to set limits on what I should receive. I believe that whatever I have lost, God will restore to me tenfold.

With the help of the Creator, you can do things that go beyond yourself when you rely on Him. The Bible says that you can soar like an eagle. An eagle is a fearless bird that will not surrender to its prey. To soar, you must not give up when you experience struggles but find a way to rise above your difficulties. When you continue to go above the turbulences of life, you will soar and experience breakthroughs. Choose to soar to manifest your dreams.

Practicing Gratitude

Gratitude is a good practice to help you focus and appreciate your present moment. Despite challenges occurring around you, practicing gratitude can help you rise above them. You should practice gratitude for your past relationship because through it, you learned about yourself and became more resilient. You can also be grateful for your singleness this season because you can take the time to heal and grow in anticipation of finding love again. Practicing gratitude will lift your spirit and help you to find the joy you have within. It will help you appreciate God's beauty around you and the people who support you no matter what.

Gratitude creates an atmosphere of peace and contentment. Whenever I intentionally write in my journal, it reminds me to appreciate all the blessings I am experiencing. If I don't document the things and people I am grateful for each day, I can miss seeing the blessings I receive. I remember reading one of my past journals. I was in awe that even the most minor things became significant as I read it. It was a reminder of my many blessings.

Focusing on what you are grateful for today teaches you to appreciate your circumstances because you know the season won't last forever. Appreciate everything and everyone around you. When you practice gratitude daily, you can show gratitude for the person God will bring to your life. You will then see God's manifestation in your life.

Seasons of Change

You experience different seasons in your life, and a relationship breakup is a difficult one to get through. You will learn that each season does not last forever.

Autumn Season

The autumn season symbolizes harvest and abundance, but it also represents the shedding of areas of your life that need to be released. Just as leaves fall off trees and mornings and evenings are darker and colder, this season represents a transition in your life. It also represents the beauty of colorful leaves and hues. This may convey the ending of a relationship that needs to be left behind and an appreciation of the lessons learned now that it has ended. Autumn is a time to reflect on your experiences; learning to be present is an essential ritual this season. Practicing meditation, journaling your thoughts, and engaging in prayer are other rituals to support the experience of change in your life. Even though it can be challenging to let go of a relationship that no longer serves you, finding the courage to let go and release the pain is critical in this season. The fallen leaves remind you that nothing is permanent in your life, and you must learn to accept change. The autumn colors will eventually be gone and will be replaced with the winter season. This is when real healing occurs.

Winter Season

I have always said I want to retire in a state with continual warmth all year. I have always enjoyed the spring and summer seasons. I can be more active in warmer weather. Even though I enjoy the changing leaves in the fall here in Virginia, I often dread that fall will turn to winter. The saving grace of winter for me is looking forward to Christmas. I enjoy spending time with family members each year.

The winter season represents cold and harsh weather. The darkness also brings seasonal depression for some people. When you experience the winter season in your life, it can be difficult to go through. If you are in this season, you may feel alone, sad, broken, and afraid. Remember that it will eventually end. It's a time to be still and quiet before the Creator to be cared for and renewed. Winter can be a season of healing and introspection. It allows you to replenish to be ready for the spring.

Spring Season

As we move from winter to spring, new seeds grow and new life springs forth. It's a time of starting over and a time of reawakening and renewal. Your life is similar. When you go through the struggles of ending a relationship and take the time to heal during the winter, spring represents a time of planting new seeds and opening your heart to love again. Just as you must water the soil for seeds to grow, you must keep watering your mind with the hope that the right partner is on the horizon. When doubt creeps in, remind yourself that you deserve pure and true love so you will live your life with expectancy and fullness until it occurs. You are in a season of waiting for the buds of love to appear. In this season, you will not accept counterfeits. You have to be intentional and not settle for someone unsuitable for you just because you might feel lonely. You must wait for the buds to be in full bloom.

Summer Season

I must admit that even though it's usually very hot outside during the summer months, this is my favorite season. I enjoy summer because the daytime hours are longer, and I enjoy seeing children playing outside and more people taking walks in the evenings. I enjoy spending time at the lake, going to festivals, and attending many outdoor activities.

Summer represents life and new opportunities. It's when you celebrate all the work that has been done to get to this season of your life. The summer season of a relationship comes when your heart is ready to receive love. It's when you are prepared to let your guard down and open your heart to give and receive love in return. It is manifested when you have healed the wounds of the previous relationship. You are now experiencing a self-love that reminds you that you are worthy to receive someone who knows your worth. Finding love brings feelings of happiness and peace. You can celebrate the manifestation of your desires to be connected to the person you hoped and prayed to be in your life.

Fifteen Green Flags in a Relationship

When you have gone through your seasons and are ready to love again, you should look for healthy signs in your new relationship that make you want to move forward. Just as you should be aware of red flags, you should also be mindful of green flags in your relationship. Green and red flags are opposites. Remember that red flags are warning signs that indicate that problems exist in a relationship and may continue into the future; green flags are signs that a healthy relationship exists and it's okay to keep pursuing your partner. Here are examples of fifteen green flags to look out for when you meet a potential partner.

1. *Similar Value Systems*

Having a similar value system means you share similar beliefs about the world. These are beliefs and principles that you live by. Examples of value systems may include living with integrity, being honest, and honoring commitments. It involves knowing your core values and connecting with someone whose values are similar to yours. Your core values should guide you in your relationship. If you meet someone who does not hold similar values, it can be detrimental to a long-term, successful relationship. Identifying your core values is critical to a healthy, thriving relationship.

One of my top core values is to maintain honesty in a relationship. If my partner is not honest, then I lose trust. If trust issues arise, then the relationship is not able to thrive.

2. *Healed Past Traumas*

You often bring past traumas into your adult relationships. However, when you are in a new relationship where you and your partner have both healed past traumas, this is a green flag. You know when healing has occurred when you can talk about your past relationships positively. This includes relationships with romantic partners, family members, and friends. Even though you have experienced deep hurt in the past, when forgiveness has occurred, anger and resentment can be released from your life. Therefore, conversations about people in the past are not spoken maliciously. You will share experiences and lessons you learned from them.

I remember talking to a gentleman who wanted to pursue me. After our first conversation, he spoke for about an hour about how awful his ex-wife was to him. I quickly realized that he had not yet worked through forgiving her for her part in the relationship's demise. He also did not take any responsibility for how he contributed to the relationship breakdown. I decided that this man was not ready to love again, and I chose not to pursue the relationship further.

You know someone has done the work when one can communicate his or her story in a healthy way because there is forgiveness for the relationship's demise and changes have been made to heal.

3. *Mutual Respect*

When you are in a new relationship, you should ensure that mutual respect exists. This involves high regard for someone's feelings, wishes, rights, or traditions. Your new partner should value your time, interests, profession, and you as a person. You can express your desires, and your partner can respect your needs.

Therefore, if you don't feel comfortable with something that is asked of you, then your partner should not force you to do it. If you have arranged to meet at a specific time, the partner should show up on time or contact you to explain why it doesn't work. Mutual respect must flow in both directions. Both individuals must know that they are respected in the relationship. Couples who respect and see each other as equals must have a healthy relationship. Respect is maintained when boundaries are expressed early in the relationship. If boundaries are broken, both parties can engage in healthy communication to restore mutual respect. Shared power shows balance in the relationship and leads to increased connection. When couples see each other as equals, they treat each other respectfully and work toward agreement when there is conflict.

4. *Honesty in the Relationship*

Dishonesty in a relationship has always been a deal breaker for me. Often, someone fears being honest in a relationship because he or she does not want to be judged by the other person. However, it is a green flag when your partner is honest with past and present experiences and feelings. Having honesty as a core value and ensuring both of you communicate honesty regardless of the outcome is critical to a healthy relationship. When you both lay the foundation of honesty, it will help build trust and confidence. Always establish this as a ground rule when you are building a relationship. Always practice being non-judgmental, remembering that no one is perfect. This approach will encourage honesty and trust in your relationship as it grows and develops.

5. *Healthy Communication*

Another green flag is healthy communication. We learned earlier about the importance of active listening and learning to validate and empathize with your partner to communicate well. Being in a relationship in which your partner uses positive and uplifting words is essential. How your new partner speaks to you early on indicates the words he or she will continue to use as the relationship grows. If your partner can use constructive words even in conflict, it's an indication of good control over his or her emotions during crises. Is your partner able to work through conflict without exiting the relationship? Can he or she speak calmly and express words of love and affirmation during conflict? Is the conversation free-flowing and easy during times of non-conflict?

Are you both invested in carving out time to listen and to understand each other's needs? Healthy communication takes practice. Most relationships fail without it. When both individuals are invested in practicing regular and safe communication, it is a green flag for a healthy relationship.

6. *Relationship Interdependence*

In a relationship, you learn to rely on each other for support. If you have been independent and have been making all decisions on your own, you must learn the importance of partnership. If you are independent, you rely on yourself; however, when you are interdependent, you will make the conscious decision to accommodate the needs of your partner. You both learn to meet each other's needs. You don't lose yourself in the relationship; you recognize the need to work as a team. You build trust when you realize you don't have to go through this life alone. Even if your partner lets you down, since no one is perfect, you can work it out together if you depend on each other to grow and maintain a sense of self. You will have the freedom to make decisions together and will not be afraid to rely on each other for support.

7. *Dedication of Time*

To get to know your new partner, there must be a dedication of time to get to know each other. Your relationship will grow if your partner creates the time to get to know you. Even if you both have hectic schedules, you'll be committed to talk regularly and enjoy activities together.

I remember being interested in getting to know someone new, but our schedules were challenging to sync together due to family and work responsibilities and illnesses. However, since we were both invested in getting to know each other, we committed to talking on the phone and texting every day until we could connect in person. The shared time talking with each other was invaluable. We learned a lot about each other's past, present, and future dreams. The time we took to connect grew our relationship organically.

When you are in a new relationship, and your partner is committed to investing in spending time to get to know you, it is a green flag because it will create a bond that will be long-lasting.

8. *Fun in the Relationship*

Relationships can thrive when couples take part in fun activities together. Even when partners have different interests, they can learn something new if they are interested in participating in an activity together. This can include a high-energy activity such as dancing, skydiving, or hiking. Low-energy activities may consist of going to a movie theater, a comedy club, a poetry event, or watching a television show at home. Regardless, each must agree to engage in the activities that bring the other partner joy and be open to trying activities that are new to one or both of them. Identifying activities that are fun for you and asking your partner to express what he or she likes to do is an excellent way to communicate needs in a relationship. Having your relationship filled with excitement and laughter keeps the relationship fun and allows you to maintain a connection.

9. *Spiritually Aligned*

When you are spiritually aligned with your partner, you'll have similar beliefs about God and your reason for being. This brings a feeling of oneness outside of your physical connection. You believe that God has brought you together for a purpose bigger than you can understand. You'll have a strong sense that you are understood and accepted for who you are, and you can provide this acceptance in return. A magnetic energy draws you together that is difficult to explain. It's easy to be vulnerable with your partner because you don't fear being judged. You may both decide to engage in spiritual practices such as praying or attending church together to strengthen the relationship. Committing to love unconditionally and giving each other grace during a relationship conflict will also help maintain a strong spiritual connection. Sharing a spiritual experience with your partner can create a strong bond that is not easily broken.

10. *Relationship Safety*

Feeling safe in your relationship is an important green flag to know if you should move forward in a new relationship. Are you free to be yourself? Are you able to express your emotions without feeling afraid or judged? Do you feel respected in your relationship? Do you feel emotionally, mentally, and physically safe with your partner? These are important questions to ask in the beginning phase of a new relationship and before you proceed in it. Trust your intuition and slow down to reflect on what you see and feel. You have now learned too much about yourself and what a healthy relationship entails; therefore, safety in your relationship is needed for it to be healthy. When you feel safe with your partner, you can work on developing your emotional attachment, which is the level of closeness you feel toward your partner. Developing emotional attachment allows you to be vulnerable with each other. As a result, you can work on communicating and remain emotionally close to your partner. You deserve a safe relationship and should not settle for anything less. Always check to see that you are emotionally, mentally, and physically safe.

11. *Commitment to Grow*

Both you and your partner intentionally putting in the work to make your relationship grow is another vital sign of a green flag. When you are in a new relationship, and you both desire to create time for each other, to communicate regularly, to understand each other's love language, and to find fun activities to engage in, the relationship will grow. Whatever time you put in is what you will get out of it. The time you invest will help you grow together emotionally, socially, physically, and spiritually. It will help when conflicts arise because both individuals are invested in seeing the relationship grow and thrive. You'll also identify the resources needed to get through rough patches. The commitment to overcome obstacles to develop the relationship is often due to the belief that it is worth fighting for because it is significant to both individuals.

12. *Kindness to Others*

Does your partner treat others with compassion? Even though he or she may have been kind to you when you initially met and continued to be so, it's equally important to observe how your partner treats other family members, friends, acquaintances, and strangers. Kindness comes from within; if your partner is naturally kind, you will see this behavior in every interaction. Kindness demonstrated in words and deeds is a green flag in a relationship. It is also reciprocal. When you are kind, others will be kind to you because it spreads. You will also give to others without the expectation of getting something in return. In your relationship, if you are giving and your partner is appreciative and continually thinking about your needs and giving to you, the relationship will grow.

13. *Relationship Chemistry*

Chemistry in a relationship can be difficult to describe. Relationship coach Jaime Bronstein defines it as "an energetic connection you can feel." It is usually due to serotonin and dopamine, the "feel-good" chemicals released in the brain when two individuals fall in love with each other. It's usually the first stage of love, called the infatuation phase. Although not everyone involved in a committed relationship has instant chemistry, it is helpful in a new relationship. You know you have chemistry when you feel butterflies in your belly, have sweaty palms, and are nervous about being with the person. You have the desire to be in your partner's presence and to connect on a deeper level. When you and your partner are experiencing these feelings, you'll have the natural inclination to pull down the emotional walls and grow the relationship.

14. *Inner Peace*

When you experience peace, you have no reason to strive for what you think you should have. Peace is defined as "freedom from disturbance or tranquility." You have a feeling of peace and calm when you are with your new partner. The "getting to know you" phase is free of stress. You both sense that peaceful energy and want to bask in it. You both can share your thoughts and feelings without fear of judgment. When you surrender, you can release all fear and embrace the person who is supposed to be in your life. When you stop trying to make your dreams happen, you experience peace and blessings flow. When experiencing inner peace, you know when to move forward and when to let go. It's a divine gift you will have when you align with the Creator in your relationship.

15. *Relationship Vulnerability*

You are experiencing a green flag in your new relationship when you are both willing to be vulnerable with each other. Even though you might be anxious about opening up your heart to someone new, you desire to move forward because a force is pulling you toward each other. You are ready to share your hurts and dreams. Your heart says it's okay to open up with this person, even with the risk of getting emotionally hurt. This vulnerability is not one-sided. The walls of both partners are pulled down, and your heart opens to let the other in. You realize the importance of being vulnerable to experience a healthy bond with each other. Even though you may share feelings of fear, you continue to push through to grow the bond with each other. You both choose to love as if past breakups never happened.

Part VII

Manifesting New Love

Pam's Story

The Relationship Breakdown

PAM MET HER husband, Phil, while she was living in Thailand. He was an American working and attending school there. She was young and did not know a great deal about relationships. They soon married, and she became a mother. Pam tried to be a good wife and mother. She noticed Phil often left the house without telling her where he was going. She was concerned about his lack of communication and wondered why he kept his whereabouts a secret. She soon learned that Phil was having an affair, and she felt hurt and angry. He did not show remorse for his behavior, so Pam left the marriage. She struggled financially as a single mother, but she was determined to make it on her own with her son. The divorce and child custody agreement was a complicated process. Pam became very angry when her ex-husband

and his family were mean to her. She had to pay child support to Phil when he refused to work. She worked minimum-wage jobs and had to survive with her child.

Pam eventually remarried. Her second husband was a good man, and they also had a son together. However, the marriage did not last because he was in constant conflict with his ex-wife. His past baggage impacted their relationship because the ex-wife exhibited threatening behavior. Pam realized that she needed to take the time to be alone and not focus on being in a relationship. She went through a second divorce and then took care of herself and both of her sons. She decided that it was time to heal.

The Healing Process

Pam's healing came in the form of meditation. She decided to meditate every day to quiet her spirit. She realized she needed to forgive her first husband so she could heal and make better choices in new relationships. She became more in tune with herself and her needs. Pam decided to also focus on her career and developed a vision to end her minimum-paying jobs. Over time, her anger dissipated. She realized that she no longer carried the pain of her failed marriages as she focused on her needs and worked on her healing through daily meditation. Pam matured into the woman she wanted to be and was no longer interested in compromising what she needed to experience joy.

Finding Love Again

As Pam focused on herself and became content with being alone, she was introduced to her third husband through a friend. She initially did not think he would be her husband because he was older, and she did not initially experience chemistry when they first met. However, she realized he had a loving and kind heart when they went on their first date. They had a lot in common with each other, and they connected on various levels. She felt drawn to him and desired to be with him. They eventually decided that they wanted to get married because their connection grew. Pam was ready to open her heart to love again because she better understood herself and her needs. She is now happily married and can successfully navigate conflict that arises in her relationship due to her self-awareness.

Lessons Learned

Pam learned that she had to trust her instinct and to honor her needs. She knew the importance of self-care through meditation. She realized that she deserved the best, and she learned to not remain in a relationship that did not meet her needs. Pam discovered that it takes courage to move on even when she felt alone in the process. She discovered her strength by moving through her fears. She became resilient amid adversity and found the strength to live fully.

Tanya's Story

The Relationship Breakdown

Tanya married George when she was twenty and he was twenty-two years old. They were married for eighteen years and had two children. George was in the military, so he traveled overseas frequently. Tanya had fun in her marriage, and they had a good beginning. But the relationship eventually failed because they had different ideas of how they should live their lives, and their different beliefs caused them to grow apart. Tanya tried to help her spouse work on himself, but she soon got tired of doing so. As they grew apart, neither one of them could sustain their marriage. George eventually had an affair; however, since Tanya had already released him emotionally over four years, it was much easier to walk away.

The Healing Process

Tanya had to deconstruct her relationship so she could heal. She asked herself, "What was my role in the breakup of my marriage?" She retraced her steps to determine what she could do differently in her next relationship. She evaluated herself to determine her role in the demise of her marriage. Tanya also began to explore if religiosity could have been part of the problem since her faith played a significant role in her expectations. In her self-exploration, she realized that it was vital for her to learn how to be alone and still be happy. She had to recognize her worth so no one could mistreat her. Tanya realized she was trying to control everything in her life, which impacted her relationships. She became self-aware and let go of the fear of being alone. She also learned the importance of not controlling someone else's life.

Finding Love Again

Tanya knew that she was ready to love again when she understood the lessons she had to learn and made herself available to receive love. She was now wiser and was looking for a different caliber of man who could be a partner with her. She was more aware of "red flags" in new relationships, which enabled her to release potential partners who were not right for her. She also envisioned a relationship in which she could have fun and be happy. When she finally met her current husband, she knew he was the one because she was ready to be in a relationship again. Tanya allows her partner to be himself rather than try to get him to conform to her desires.

Lessons Learned

Tanya learned the importance of maintaining communication to make her current marriage work. She also learned the importance of having regular date nights to maintain a connection with her husband. She also learned the importance of checking in with each other to make sure that they are doing well emotionally. To build a marriage that is strong and anchored, Tanya and her husband eat dinner, pray, and attend online church as a couple. Tanya learned the importance of releasing

Manifesting New Love

control and attracting a soulmate who believed in being an equal partner in the marriage.

Cassie's Story

The Relationship Breakdown

Cassie struggled in her relationship with her ex-husband. She was hurt when she found out he was unfaithful. She worked hard to salvage the marriage because of her Christian faith. She did not want to lose her family, and she grew up believing that divorce was not an option. Her family encouraged her to try to restore it. Cassie stayed because she thought she was the reason that her spouse cheated. Being in this marriage environment affected her self-esteem and her feelings of self-worth. She tried to fight for it, but her husband decided he did not want to remain in the marriage.

The Healing Process

This was a difficult season in Cassie's life. She had to mourn the marriage and rely on God to get through the breakup. She learned to surrender her struggles to God and submit her will to Him. She attended a divorce and recovery group to help her get through it. She relied on

143

a women's support group to encourage her in her dark periods.

Cassie had to examine what she brought into the marriage that was not working for her. She had no example of a healthy relationship when she was growing up. She also did not have a healthy role model from her father. As an adult, she had no support from her family through her relationship struggles, which contributed to her feeling alone. Cassie spent four years focusing on caring for herself while going through her divorce. She took classes to build herself up spiritually and read self-help books on how to have a healthy marriage. She changed her diet and exercised regularly. She also went out with friends without focusing on dating. She scheduled time to be alone to connect with God. Most of all, Cassie decided that she would learn to forgive her ex-spouse and pray for him. The divorce process was tedious and stressful because of the custody fight over the children. The more she felt free and began to heal, the easier it became to forgive her ex-husband.

Finding Love Again

Cassie felt ready to date more than four years after separating from her ex-husband. She finally met her second husband after being clear about the type of relationship she wanted. The dating process took work, and her heart was broken numerous times.

When Cassie met her current husband, he was different. He was kind, open, spiritually centered, and financially responsible. He cared for his body, and he was active with his children. They prayed together daily and did online Bible study together. Cassie realized after pouring out her heart to God to bless her with love again, He chose this man to be in her life. She knew she had a lot to offer him. She feels that God chose them for each other. Cassie now knows her worth and is grateful for this relationship. She is constantly learning and growing with her new husband.

Lessons Learned

Cassie needed to find herself and to understand her worth. She also learned to take time for herself and to enjoy being alone. She knew the importance of connecting with God and trusting that He had a plan for her and her children. She set boundaries with her family when she realized they were not supporting her. Cassie understood the importance of caring for her body, mind, and spirit. She spent time connecting with God and others to aid in the recovery process. She has learned that she can be in a healthy relationship because she is now emotionally healthy.

Evelyn's Story

The Relationship Breakdown

Evelyn was married to a military man at age nineteen. Due to traveling responsibilities in the military, their lack of maturity, and different life goals, they grew apart. They realized they did not have the skills to work on their differences. They did not know how to communicate effectively, and their conflict turned into a blame game. Evelyn felt that neither of them could see each other's assets in the marriage. Although she knew her husband cared about her, Evelyn thought he was not committed. After over eight years of marriage, she decided to end the relationship.

Evelyn soon met another man who had the motivation to improve his life. He was career-oriented with a high-status position and was motivated to achieve new endeavors in his life. Evelyn was attracted to him, but she realized he could not meet her needs emotionally. He was focused on himself and was not family-oriented or committed to her. He was involved in inappropriate relationships with other women while they were together. Unfortunately, when Evelyn recognized these negative qualities, she was already in love with him. When she became pregnant, she found the courage to leave the relationship. She did not want her son to grow up in a dysfunctional household with a man who would not commit to her. When the relationship ended, Evelyn focused on working on herself and caring for her son.

Healing Process

Evelyn felt that she was not interested in getting married again. She wanted to take her focus off of dating and turn her attention to working on herself. She took the time to better understand her choices in relationships and why she made the decisions she did. She mourned her relationship losses and accepted responsibility for her actions.

Evelyn had to be honest about her true desires. She desired a relationship with a man who knew how to love and who would be attuned to her needs. She worked on forgiving herself for her choices and for the guilt and shame of being a single mother. She grew up believing she had to have an intact family. Evelyn learned to affirm herself by saying, "Failed relationships are a part of my story; however, it's not who I am." She also reminded herself that there are no mistakes in the universe, but there are only lessons that provide an opportunity to grow. She affirms that she is good and God's masterpiece.

Evelyn decided to date again and to be in a place of vulnerability. She became honest with herself about what she wanted in a relationship and became clear about whether or not a man could meet her needs. She knew she was ready when she was able to release her guilt and shame and become honest with herself.

Finding Love Again

Evelyn met her new husband through online dating. She knew this gentleman was the one because he embodied the positive traits of both of her previous lovers. He was committed, loving, kind, educated, and career-driven, and he adored her. Evelyn also noticed that he was self-reflective when they experienced conflict. She had to tune in to her emotional responses when there was conflict to receive the effect she desired. After the first date, they connected every day.

They learned to be vulnerable with each other. Evelyn opened up her heart to love again and married her soulmate. They have been married for thirteen years, and they practice how to communicate effectively with each other. They enjoy spending time together and invest in experiences that build the relationship. They attend church and pray together and are couples' ministry leaders. They are both committed to making their marriage work.

Lessons Learned

Evelyn learned the importance of assessing her role in her two relationship breakups and taking responsibility for her actions. She worked on letting go of guilt and shame for ending a relationship to raise her child as a single mother. She understood the significance of identifying her needs and desires. She understood that settling for someone who could not emotionally commit to a relationship would deny her the blessings God had for her. She could communicate her worth by leaving relationships that no longer served her. Evelyn gained clarity about what she wanted when she took the time to do her work. This allowed her to open her heart to love again. She was able to find a husband who embodied the characteristics she desired.

Hold On to Hope

What if you have done your work and you are waiting for your purpose partner or soulmate to appear, but it still has not happened? The stories highlighted are perfect examples of how your purpose partner can be manifested after broken relationships. These are ordinary people who worked through their healing and prepared their hearts to love again while being in a place of surrender. I encourage you to continue to hold on to hope that your heart's desires can be manifested, too. It would be great to look into a mirror to see the date and time this person will appear; however, like other desires, we cannot predict the future. We must learn to let go of areas we can't control and live in faith in complete surrender.

When you believe that your dreams will be manifested, you will not need to strive or doubt that this will happen. Learning to step out in faith and live your life to the fullest will create opportunities to connect with others. You can continue to enjoy your life in the waiting, to be grateful for all your experiences, and to accept your circumstances today. Continue to live your life, anticipating all that is coming your way. It's essential to keep your heart open to give and receive love until your season comes. You are an overcomer of all your brokenness. Even more important is remembering that you are whole and you are loved!

Afterword

LOOKING BACK AT my life, I realized I needed to go through heartbreak to learn to rely on God for my healing. The years of darkness after my relationship and subsequent divorce seemed never-ending. I had a difficult time seeing the light through my tunnel vision. I am grateful for God's infinite love. I took the time to heal, learn, and be reminded that I am not alone. I learned to trust Him that my future would be brighter and better than what I lost. I learned to use my wisdom and knowledge as a psychotherapist to help others who have experienced the loss of their relationships.

My inspiration to write this book is the desire to reach many more people I ordinarily would not meet to tell them that there is healing after a heartbreak. The message of hope is infused in this book. My past experiences, including my wounds, made me introspective to understand the importance of healing better. I chose to be intentional to do the work and understand my pain to heal and thrive. I had to work on my mind, body, and spirit to heal the broken pieces of my life and create space for my purpose partner who would manifest.

On this healing journey, I learned to open my heart to give and receive love again. I have learned to discern the type of relationship that is right for me based on the value system of my partner, his love for God, and how he treats me. I can sense when it's time to open my heart or when it's time to walk away. When the internal and external work was completed, I knew I was ready to open my heart to love again.

I am sharing my insight to help others heal and attract the right partner. Healthy people radiate a bright light to attract healthy partners. I pray that this book provides insight and hope that healing can happen after the loss of a romantic relationship and that you will find love again if your heart remains open. Remember, there is life after brokenness.

9 798989 778447